the Road to Rockliffe

Published in November 2010 by The Northern Echo, Priestgate, Darlington, County Durham DL1 1NF. The Northern Echo is part of Newsquest (Yorkshire and North-East) Ltd which is a Gannett company.

Website: www.northernecho.co.uk
Email: chris.lloyd@nne.co.uk
Text copyright © The Northern Echo 2010

All rights reserved. No part of this publication may be reproduced, stored in a retrieval system, or transmitted, in any form or by any means (electronic, mechanical, photocopying, recording or otherwise) without the prior written permission of the publishers
The author asserts the moral right to be identified as the author of this work

British Library Cataloguing in Publication Data
A catalogue record for this book is available from the British Library
ISBN 0-978-0-9555931-2-3

Printed by the University of Northumbria

Rockliffe Hall
Hurworth-on-Tees, Darlington, County Durham DL2 2DU
01325-729999
Website: www.rockliffehall.com
Email: enquiries@rockliffehall.com

Cover design: Jeff Dixon at Jigsaw Design Studios Ltd, Newcastle
Website: www.jigsaw-design.com

The Road to Rockliffe

by Chris Lloyd

ROCKLIFFE HALL

The Northern Echo

Contents

Foreword   5

Part I: The Road to Rockliffe

   1: Road, River and Romans   7
   2: Skelly of Seringapatam   12
   3: Weaving the Loop Together   17
   4: The Age of the Train   27
   5: Introducing Mr Backhouse   34
   6: The Botanical Backhouses   41
   7: Project Pilmore   46
   8: The Great Darlington Frog   55
   9: Woodland Beauties   61
   10: The Illegal Member and the Pharoah's Daughter   71
   11: The Captain, the Colonel and the Lord   90
   12: Pomegranates and Prayers   99
   13: Erimus   105

Part II: Along the Road to Rockliffe

   14: Croft Spa   113
   15: Croft Church   118
   16: Lewis Carroll   122
   17: Croft Bridge   128
   18: Hell's Kettles   134
   19: Sir Ernest Cassel   136
   20: Comet   141
   21: Old Hurworth   148
   22: William Emerson   156
   23: Drink   161
   24: Low Hail Bridge   165
   25: Newbus   167
   26: Neasham and the Headless Hobgoblin   169
   27: Sockburn and the Dragon   174

Acknowledgements   182
Bibliography and Index   183

Foreword

I REMEMBER my first time coming down the drive to Rockliffe. On one side, Middlesbrough Football Club had created a state-of-the-art training complex on top of the ridge overlooking the river. On the other side, hidden behind a screen of trees and in danger of being lost almost entirely to creeping ivy, was an old, dark, derelict hall.

Despite its hotch-potch of out-buildings and the remains of its previous life as a hospital, the empty hall had an air of faded grandeur about it, particularly when I walked into what had been the formal pleasuregardens and looked out across the fields towards the Tees. Indeed, there was a feeling coming down the years that this had once been someone's pride and joy, and that every planting in the park and every finial on the roofline had been someone's intricate planning. The hall also had an air of defiance, a determination that it would not be defeated by the passage of time. I hope that in turning it into a grand hotel, adding a spa and designing a golf course in its grounds we have helped it win its victory and given it a new lease of life.

This book tells of the long journey that started with the Romans, was given great direction by the Victorian banker Alfred Backhouse and has ended with the creation of the hotel. In that respect, it tells of the road to Rockliffe.

But, hopefully for the interest of visitors and local residents alike, it tells of some of the fascinating stories that helped shape this district in days gone by. From a grinning cat to a fire-breathing dragon – with a wonderful Waterhouse mansion in between – all these stories can be found along the road to Rockliffe.

I hope you enjoy the journey.

Warwick Brindle
Chairman, Rockliffe Hall Ltd

Warwick Brindle, right, with Rockliffe Hall managing director Nick Holmes

Part I:
The Road to Rockliffe

Rockliffe Hall was known to its Quaker creator Alfred Backhouse as plain Pilmore. This 1930s photograph shows the superb east elevation looking over the formal gardens with one of Alfred's specimen fir trees enhancing the picture

1: Road, River and Romans

THE Rockliffe road runs with barely a deviation through villages lapped by the tea-brown Tees. It runs as straight as a die, which is in contrast to the ponderous meanderings of the nearby river which flows to all four points of the compass, giving the district its character, its boundaries, its large loops and, of course, its rocky cliffs.

The river begins its progress high on the peaty Pennine moors. At first it is a rapid progress, tearing through upper Teesdale, sculpting stone cathedrals out of hard whinstone and plunging without a prayer over High Force – England's mightiest, and most famous, waterfall.

In those early stages, it is a river that knows its mind, a ribbon rushing south-east between steep tree-lined banks and grassy green pastures, not stopping to stare at the silhouettes on its cliffs, the tumbledown ruins of castles and abbeys.

Gradually, though, the river loses its sense of purpose, its push of progress. Directional doubts creep in and it gains the characteristic which caused ancient people to christen it Taoi – Celtic for winding.

Its windings around south-east Darlington are broad and sweeping, but as it approaches Croft-on-Tees – where the straight road past Rockliffe begins – it becomes schizophrenic and sinuous. Instead of flowing to the coast, it snakes suddenly south. Quickly realising the error of its way, it turns east again before spinning round west and then heading north. These windings of uncertainty create a grand loop of low-lying pasture on the Durham side and pile up a steep, scrabbly cliff on the Yorkshire bank – "a raw cliff" which gives its name to the low-lying pasture within the loop.

High Force

As it swings east once more, the Tees reaches into the heart of Hurworth – Hurdewurda, "the wood by the water" – and having washed the feet of the church, it turns its snaking into a squiggling. It performs a curious kink around Newbus and slinks in the shape of a nose past Neasham – "the estate on the nose-shaped bend".

Then the river turns up its nose at County Durham and plunges southwards, miles deep into Yorkshire. But it doesn't like what it sees and abruptly changes its mind. It flows directly north, creating a finger-thin sliver of land known as the Sockburn peninsula. Up, up to Low Dinsdale it flows before performing a large circumnavigation in front of Middleton One Row. The clifftop houses in the one row give it an ovation, standing with a magnificent view spread out before them.

7

The Road to Rockliffe

Hurworth from the Ring Field, with the winding Tees sweeping in front of the church

That, though, is the Tees' final flourish. As it leaves Low Middleton, it starts to recover its sense of direction. It now knows where it is heading – the coast – and knows how to get there: north-east. Because old habits die hard, there are still a few wayward windings that it really should have been ironed out – indeed, 19th Century man did iron them out in Middlesbrough by cutting canals across the loops so that ships laden with coal could reach the sea more quickly, and profitably.

By the time the Tees flows past the Riverside Stadium, the home of Middlesbrough Football Club, it is broad and true. It is as if, 85 miles after its beginnings, it has finally reconciled itself with its fate and it yields its browny, peaty waters to the anonymous enormity of the North Sea.

Yet these winding habits have created a district of great character. For instance, Sockburn's peninsula pushes so deeply into Yorkshire that, with the river curving almost completely around it, the sliver feels cut off from the rest of the world. It is enveloped in an isolated calm in which ancient man found spiritual peace. He built a little chapel which had such sacred significance in the 8th Century that bishops were crowned there. But the peace was destroyed by a terrible poison-breathing dragon until a brave knight, Sir John Conyers, slayed it with his enormous sword. His remains are entombed in stone in the chapel, his effigy carved boldly on his coffin lid showing that he is still embroiled in the battle between good and evil.

A couple of miles eastwards – of course, that's a couple of miles eastwards as the straight-forward crow flies but not as the meandering Tees flows – a similar feeling of heavenly solitude amid water and wood can be found on the grand loop of Rockliffe. It was sustenance of a more earthly kind that attracted the first people to quit their nomadic lifestyle and settle inside the low-lying loop. The fertile soil, frequently topped up with nutrients by the river's regular floods, provided fine agricultural land for growing crops.

In the early summer of 2007, when work on the golf course was beginning, archaeologists discovered evidence of a short-lived Roman settlement on a riverside field on the eastern edge of the Rockliffe loop. These finds suggest a domestic, rural way of life in the early 4th Century. There were three Romano-British corn-drying kilns, fragments of a Roman millstone, possibly imported from Derbyshire, and a heavy piece of a quernstone – a corn hand-grinder. It was probably locally-made from an erratic rock – a rock which during the last Ice Age 80,000 years ago had hitched a ride on a glacier from Shap Fell, on the Cumbrian side of the Pennines, and moved slowly down the Tees Valley, its rough edges being bumped smooth as it travelled. When the glacier melted, the rock fell to earth and stopped, never to move again – until a mere 2,000 years ago when a Roman hand picked it up and fashioned it for milling.

Erratics are fairly common along the Tees – a large rounded one, usually iced with white duck droppings, can be seen in the middle of the river near the site of Rockliffe's 1877 carriagebridge.

The archaeologists also found two quenching troughs for a nearby forge, an unusual buckle, a 4th Century Roman coin and the remains of a fine dish which had been spun on a lathe and the inside tinned with copper alloy.

But why was the Romans' stay inside such an entrancing loop so short-lived? The speculation is that they were driven

The remains of Rockliffe's Roman dish

out by floods – until reservoirs were built in upper Teesdale in the early 1970s, the Tees Bore was a sight to behold in times of rapid thaw and heavy rain. It was a wall of water six feet high spurting and spuming down the dale, inundating all in its path. In 1531, for instance, "a peerser or bore" undermined three of the "sixed myghtye large pillars" of Croft's bridge and "a great quantite" of the arches fell down. If it could do that to a bridge as sturdy as Croft's it would wreak havoc with a flimsy domestic settlement. Little wonder that, once overwhelmed, the Romans thought it prudent to settle on higher ground.

As short-lived as it was, such a Roman domestic settlements are rare in south Durham. There are four others (Holme House near Piercebridge, Old Durham to the south-east of Durham City, and Faverdale to the north of Darlington) with the

The Road to Rockliffe

An 1866 etching of the ancient bridge over the River Tees at Croft

nearest no more than half-a-mile away. Two villas have been found at Dalton-on-Tees, which is directly across the river and up the rocky cliff – high enough to escape the Tees Bore. It is a tantalizing thought: did the Romans wade from one settlement to the other across the Tees at the spot where Alfred Backhouse built his carriagebridge 1,600 years later?

That brief flirtation with the Romans was the only excitement within the Rockliffe loop for a millennium and more. Gradually, the farmers worked out the waterline and shared out the pastureland above it between them. By the end of the 18th Century, there were five farms within the loop: Hurworth Grange, Pilmore Farm, Pilmore House, High Rawcliff and Rawcliff.

The farms of Rawcliff were closest to the river. They were beneath the Rawcliff Scaur – the river's cliff on the eastern bend of the loop. It wasn't a rocky cliff, as you might imagine. It was a raw cliff. The river washed by it, keeping the soil tumbling down it so that few plants or trees could get a foothold. Consequently, the cliff was forever open or naked: it was a cliff that was in the raw.

Those farms at Pilmore, where today's hotel is, had adopted a fashionably bleak-sounding name although the nearest moorland was Brackin Moor or Hurworth Moor to the north, between the village of Hurworth and the town of Darlington.

It is likely that Hurworth Grange, the most easterly of the five and now beneath Middlesbrough FC's training complex, was originally the principal farm. A grange usually started off as a grain store connected to an ecclesiastical establishment such as an abbey or a priory, and down the straight road in Neasham, a small Benedictine priory was established in the mid-12th Century. Among the possessions of the priory's eight nuns was a "carucate" of land – 120 acres – at Hurworth: the original Hurworth Grange?

When William Hutchinson was writing in 1794, Hurworth's properties were much of a muchness – all were equally delightful, of course, but none was outstanding enough to merit a mention in its own right. He enthused: "The village of Hurworth

Road, River and Romans

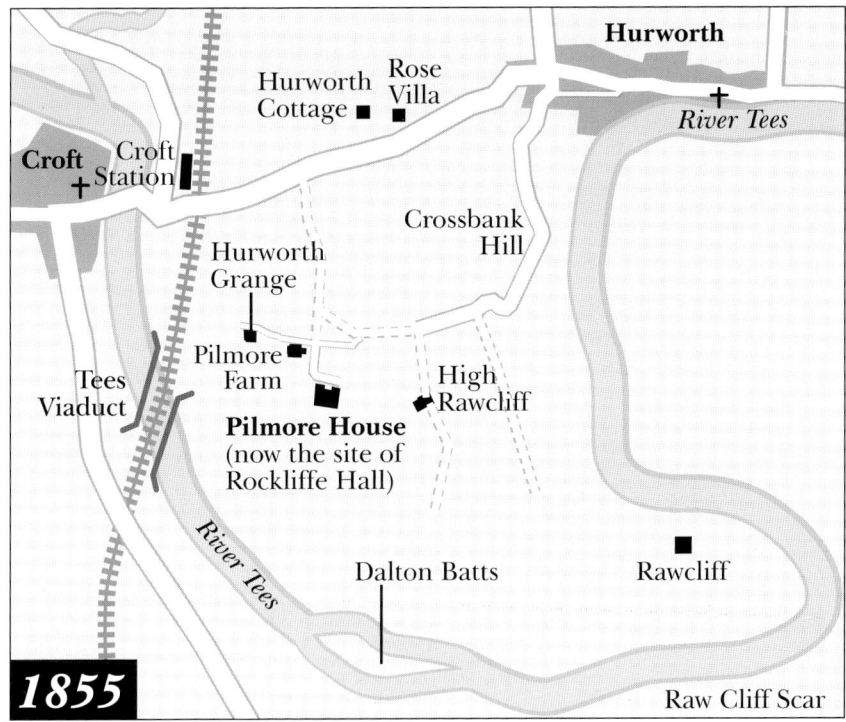

lies on the brink of a steep hill above the River Tees facing the south, and is one of the most delightful situations in the county of Durham. The village is within three miles of Darlington, and in the neighbourhood are many families of good fortune. The prospect into Yorkshire is not extensive, but beautiful; the river winds round a plain, and the opposite banks rise swiftly, forming an amphitheatre of about four miles in circumference."

Yet by the time Parson and White compiled their directory in 1828, some houses had become more equal than others. They wrote: "There are three gentlemen's villas in the township of Hurworth, viz Pilmore House (Col Gordon Skelly), Hurworth Cottage (George James Esq) and Newbus Grange (Jonathan Featherstone Esq)."

Newbus Grange is in that curious kink downstream; Hurworth Cottage is to the north of the straight road. But Colonel Gordon Skelly's Pilmore House is directly beneath Rockliffe Park. In fact, today's hotel may even be standing on his cellars, their low-vaulted ceilings made with elderly, thin, handmade red brick.

The Colonel seems to have been the first person to raise Pilmore above the respectable comfort enjoyed by the other families in the district and create a "most complete Residence for a genteel Family" which was "delightfully situated" amid the water and wood of a grand loop of the River Tees.

11

2: Skelly of Seringapatam

THE Tees sweeps around to wash the foot of the cliff at Hurworth-on-Tees on which All Saints Church has stood since Norman times. From its prominent position, the main door of the church looks south over Yorkshire, and the churchyard tumbles down the steeply unstable slope, threatening to spill the graves' contents and raise the dead.

The last resting place of Colonel Gordon Skelly, of Pilmore House, is more assured. It is in a singular position of importance, directly beneath the belltower, to the west of the main door and adjacent to the path. Everyone who has entered the church these past 200 years has marched straight past this military man.

A huge and heavy stone slab covers his vault. It is grandiloquently identified by only two deeply carved Georgian capitals: GS. Resting against the tower is a stone of a different colour and type to the vault, and apparently of a later date, which fills in the gaps between the initials. It says: "At the foot of this Stone are deposited the mortal remains of GORDON SKELLY, late a Lieutenant Colonel in the Army, in which he served many years with distinguished reputation; the attacks led by him at the last celebrated Siege of Seringapatam are particularly recorded. He departed this life the 30th day of November, 1828, aged 61 years. Also the remains of JANE, daughter of the above GORDON SKELLY and ELIZABETH his wife, who died the 8th of June, 1811, aged 5 weeks. Also of GORDON, their eldest Son, who died the 10th of November, 1821, aged 14 years."

All Saints Church, Hurworth. Col Skelly is buried on the right hand side of the tower

Skelly of Seringapatam

Colonel Skelly's large grave cover lies on the ground, with only GS carved on it. Leaning against the church is an apparently later headstone, now weathered, on which his brave deeds at Seringapatam are recorded

Time has not been kind to Colonel Skelly.

True, his vault has survived while the church around it has been twice rebuilt, in 1831 and again in 1871, so that all that remains of the original Norman construction are six pillars in the nave and part of the belltower. But the iron railings which once enclosed the war hero's vault have vanished – presumably commandeered to help fight a later war – and the inscribed headstone is crumbling to dust, its details disappearing from view just as the derring-do of the last celebrated siege of Seringapatam has faded from public consciousness.

The Colonel came from an aristocratic background. His first name was his direct connection to his paternal great-grandfather, Alexander Gordon, the 2nd Duke of Gordon. In 1707 the Duke married Lady Henrietta Mordaunt, the daughter of the 3rd Earl of Peterborough, and they had 11 children, the youngest of whom, Lady Betty Gordon, had to make do with marriage to a clergyman, the Reverend John Skelly. Their son – the Colonel's father – was Captain Gordon Skelly RN, who commanded HMS Devonshire, a 66-gun ship-of-the-line (warships lined up in an attempt to blow their opponents out of the water), with great distinction during the Seven Years War (1754-1763) in North America. In June 1758, he was involved in the siege and capture of the Fortress of Louisbourg, the French stronghold that guarded the St Lawrence River. This victory opened the way for him to take part in an attack upriver the following summer on Quebec. The French city was besieged for three months and then fell after only an hour's battle one September morning, and France's colonial era in North America came to an end.

Back home, the Captain married Dorothy, the niece of Sir Richard Perrott, the 2nd Baron Perrott of Plumstead, Kent, and their eldest son was born on June 5, 1766. Not only did he share his father's name, but he also followed in his footsteps, off to

13

The Road to Rockliffe

war to expand the British Empire. A reference in the diary of Major-General Lachlan Macquarie, "an old American friend" of Skelly Junior who became the Governor of New South Wales in Australia, suggests that as a mid-teenager, he was stationed in North America, probably in Canada. Another brief mention places Skelly in India at the first siege of Seringapatam during the Third Anglo-Mysore War of 1792. Then the Hurworth headstone trumpets that Skelly was at the second siege in 1799 which was the final battle in the Fourth Anglo-Mysore War.

There was a series of wars lasting nearly four decades at the end of the 18th Century between the Indian Kingdom of Mysore and the British East India Company. It was a conflict about commerce and influence – Mysore, and its leader Tipu Sultan, was an ally of France.

Srirangapatna – or Seringapatam as the English tongue pronounced it – was the capital of Mysore. It was a town on an island surrounded by the River Kaveri (or Cauvery, as the British said). It was dominated by the 9th Century Ranganathaswamy Temple, although the British were more interested in the jewels and great riches inside Tipu Sultan's palace.

Following the first siege of 1792, Tipu Sultan signed away half of his kingdom to the British who returned seven years later to complete the conquest. Seringapatam was besieged from mid-April 1799 until the decisive storming on May 4. Arthur Wellesley, the 30-year-old Duke of Wellington, was among the battalion commanders, and Skelly was in charge of 559 men of all ranks from the 12th, 74th and 6th regiments of the Scotch Brigade.

"The final result of this glorious and memorable Day, was, that our Troops were in Complete Possession of Tippoo Sultaun's Fortress and Capital in less than an hour from the commencement of the assault; the Sultaun himself, and a great many of his principal officers, killed in the Storm; his sons and all his Family our Prisoners; and all his immense Riches and Treasures in our Possession," wrote Lachlan Macquarie in his journal. "The loss of the enemy in killed and wounded in the Storm is very great – but cannot possibly be exactly ascertained – as they lay in such immense Heaps on the Ramparts – and in the ditch – as well as in different Parts of the Town – that no regular account of them could be taken."

Mysore was now British, and Skelly had played his part in thwarting French colonial ambitions, just like his father.

Macquarie continued his account: "Our own loss on this grand occasion – tho' comparatively very small in proportion to the magnitude of the object attained – is still very considerable; having had several very valuable officers – and great many gallant soldiers, killed and wounded in the Assault."

Of the 559 men under Skelly's command, 13 were killed and 30 wounded. He received a special mention in dispatches and an inclusion on a 2,550 square foot drawing of the battle by Sir Richard Ker Porter. "Designed from the most authentic and correct information relative to the scenery of the place, the costume of the soldiery and the various circumstances of the attacks", the painting was soon on

Sir Richard Ker Porter's view of the Siege of Seringapatam, featuring No 18, Major Gordon Skelly (right). Picture courtesy of the V&A Museum

display at the Lyceum in the Strand (admission: one shilling).

A reviewer in 1801, fearing the picture would soon be lost because of its unfeasible enormity, tried to describe it. He began: "The most striking group meets the eye in the centre of the picture. It consists of General Baird, attended by his aid-de-camps, animating and encouraging the troops, who are storming the battery; while Serjeant Graham, who has already mounted the rampart, and planted the British colours on its summit, is shot dead by an Indian, at the moment when he is giving the signal of victory. At the top of the first acclivity, Major Craigie, with the grenadiers of the 12th regiment, is directing the attack; while another party, of the 74th, under Major Skelly, are preparing to mount the battery on the left, aided by the Madras native pioneers, with scaling ladders. Captain Cormicke, a brave officer is seen falling headlong down the

15

steep, being killed near the upper part of the rampart. Halfway up the breach is a sally of Tippoo's guards, who are repulsed by the 74th regiment. Lieutenant Prendergast appears mortally wounded by a musket shot; and Lieutenant Shaw lies among the slain in the thickest groups of the battle."

One wonders if Skelly ever saw himself immortalized on the huge canvas because he was soon back in Britain. In 1800, a year after the siege, he married Elizabeth, the daughter of James Newsam of Dunsa Bank, a manor house between the North Yorkshire villages of Ravensworth and Newsham close to what is now the A66 trans-Pennine road. Dunsa is less than 20 miles from Hurworth and this proximity is the best explanation of how the hero of Seringapatam became the laird of Pilmore.

At the house, Betty and the Colonel had five children. As well as the two poor souls who died young, there were two more daughters: Elizabeth, who married Captain Colling of Haughton-le-Skerne, and Dorothy, who married the Reverend Rowland Webster. The remaining son, Francis, continued the family's military tradition, also reaching the rank of colonel and spreading the British Empire into Ceylon.

Skelly – a man of the establishment, because on November 2, 1819, he was one of 750 signatories on the County of Durham Loyal Declaration, and in March the following year, he was sworn onto the Grand Jury at the Durham Lent Assizes to sit in judgement on his peers – raised his family at Pilmore, and he raised Pilmore above the status of working farm or even comfortable villa.

He died and was laid to rest beneath his huge and heavy slab in November 1828, and on July 13, 1829, his estate was auctioned at the King's Head Inn, Darlington. The estate agent's blurb said Pilmore was now a "most desirable mansion house…surrounded by thriving Shrubberies and Plantations". It was described it as being "delightfully situated on the Banks of the River Tees, and distant about one Mile from Croft, four from Darlington, four from the much-frequented Spa, Dinsdale, eleven from Richmond, and in the immediate Neighbourhood of the Raby, Hurworth, and Sedgefield Hunts".

The description continued: "The Mansion-House comprises spacious and handsome Dining and Drawing-Rooms, Breakfast-Room, and Entrance-Hall, with suitable Bed-Rooms, Servants' Hall, Kitchens, excellent Cellars, Brew-House, Coach-House and Stables, with Hay-Lofts, Corn Chambers, and other necessary Out-Offices, also a good walled Kitchen Garden, well stocked with choice Fruit Trees, altogether forming a most complete Residence for a genteel Family.

"The Estate (on which are two substantial Farm-houses with all requisite Out-Buildings) contains 170 Acres, or thereabouts, of rich Arable, Meadow and Pasture Land, and lies in a Ring Fence."

The advertisement for the sale was placed in the Newcastle Courant and the Leeds Mercury, suggesting that the agents believed that prospective purchasers for such a rare opportunity would be drawn from far and wide. Ironically, though, the next owner was already living inside that attractive loop of the Tees.

3: Weaving the Loop Together

WHEN the "most desirable mansion house and estate" of Pilmore was presented to the regional property market in 1829, Hurworth was at its most prosperous for centuries. It had plenty of well-to-do houses, halls, villas and mansions, as J Gordon reported in his 1834 guide to the area: "Hurworth has more the appearance of an assemblage of gentlemen's seats than of an ordinary village." In the same year, E Mackenzie and M Ross in their definitive history of Durham reiterated that Pilmore was among the three choicest "gentlemen's villas" in the district.

Beyond this established wealth, Hurworth had a pleasing degree of prosperity among its labouring classes. Nearby Darlington had, for the last century or so, been a major player in the European textile market, partly because its waters were ideal for bleaching and partly because its merchants were innovative and well-organised. Hurworth piggy-backed on its neighbour's success. It put the waters of the winding Tees to good use, and also its cliffs – as the village spilled westwards beyond the church, the weavers worked in subterranean rooms dug into the riverbank. Other weavers worked in the "old barracks" opposite the church – this name appears to be a literal translation of the French "baraque", meaning hut or shed, rather than suggestive of a military connection.

Hurworth's population almost doubled in the first three decades of the 19th Century – from 661 in 1801 to 1831 in 1,017. At the start of the 1830s, about 120 handloom weavers were at work in the village, all of them male, and the road to the Darlington merchants would be crowded with Hurworth men carrying linen in packs on their backs or driving donkeys laden with heavy panniers.

"The business was prosperous," wrote Dr Thomas Dixon Walker, the village GP.

Hurworth linen weavers' properties at the east end of the village from Low Hail Bridge

The Road to Rockliffe

"By only working five days in the week, and spending the other two in dissipation, an able-bodied man could earn from twenty-five to twenty-eight shillings per week; and an apprentice to the trade earned from seven to fifteen shillings."

While the weavers were pulling Hurworth westwards, even more interesting and long-lasting developments were happening to the east in the neighbouring village of Croft-on-Tees. Since 1688, when horses drinking spring water were miraculously cured of their ailments, Croft, on the Yorkshire side of the river, had been noted as a place of recuperation. Then, in the late 1820s, the discovery of the New Well was followed by the building of the New Spa and the rebuilding of the Croft Spa Hotel, and the healthy village began turning into a spa resort capable of attracting visitors from across the country.

Part of Croft's attraction to visitors from the south was its easy-to-reach position on the Great North Road which crossed the Tees by its ancient bridge. Merchants from the north also eyed up the bridge as an important connection to the markets of North Yorkshire.

The big issue in the Darlington district in the latter half of the 18th Century was how its coal could be sold for the highest price. For centuries, coalowners had been frustrated that their black gold was located in remote areas to the east of Bishop Auckland, and the only way to get it to market was via pack ponies which plodded

The new spa at Croft which was built in the late 1820s so people could take the water

very slowly along the back lanes, more interested in cropping the grass than building up their masters' profits.

In 1767, when canalmania gripped the nation, it was proposed to build a 33-mile waterway from the Staindrop area of Teesdale through Darlington to Stockton where the coal could be loaded into bigger ships to sail down the Tees and out onto the seas. James Brindley, the foremost canal engineer in the country, drew up the plans. He included a branch of the canal that would flow for three miles and 821 chains from the heart of Darlington through a series of locks into Hurworth Place. In effect, and hard to believe, where the East Coast Mainline goes under the straight road that runs past the entrance to Rockliffe, there would have been a dock and probably a canal basin. Here the coal barges would have been unloaded by rudimentary cranes and the coal sent on its way into Yorkshire on carts and in panniers.

The 1767 canal plan was scuppered by cost and by the dear old Tees – at Stockton in those days it was so wibbly-wobbly that it was quicker to sail from London to the mouth of the river than it was from the mouth of the river into Stockton. Until a couple of cuts removed a couple of large windings of the Tees in the early 19th Century, a boat could take three weeks to navigate its meanderings into Stockton.

Although the canal plan was holed, the idea never went away. In 1818, another generation of entrepreneurs – led by local banker Jonathan Backhouse (1747-1826) – revived the idea, and their surveyor, George Overton, proposed a 35-mile railway – the Stockton and Darlington Railway (S&DR) – from the coalfield to the sea. It would have 16 miles of branchline running off it, including one to the Durham side of Croft bridge. This would enable the coal to reach the Yorkshire markets, but it obviated the need for the railwaymen to build an expensive bridge over the tempestuous Tees. Backhouse even predicted 10,000 tons of coal a year would be sold at the branch's depot, which would be behind what is today the Comet public house.

The 1767 canal plan (see also Page 20)

This time the idea gained traction. An Act of Parliament was passed on May 23, 1823, giving the railway pioneers permission to build the line, including the £74,300 three-and-a-half mile branchline.

The S&DR opened on September 27, 1825; the Croft branchline – the third of its kind in the world – opened on October 27, 1829. "Numerous coaches" each drawn by a single horse and crowded with between 30 and 50 banner-waving passengers and followed by a train of wagons filled with coal travelled along it on that opening day.

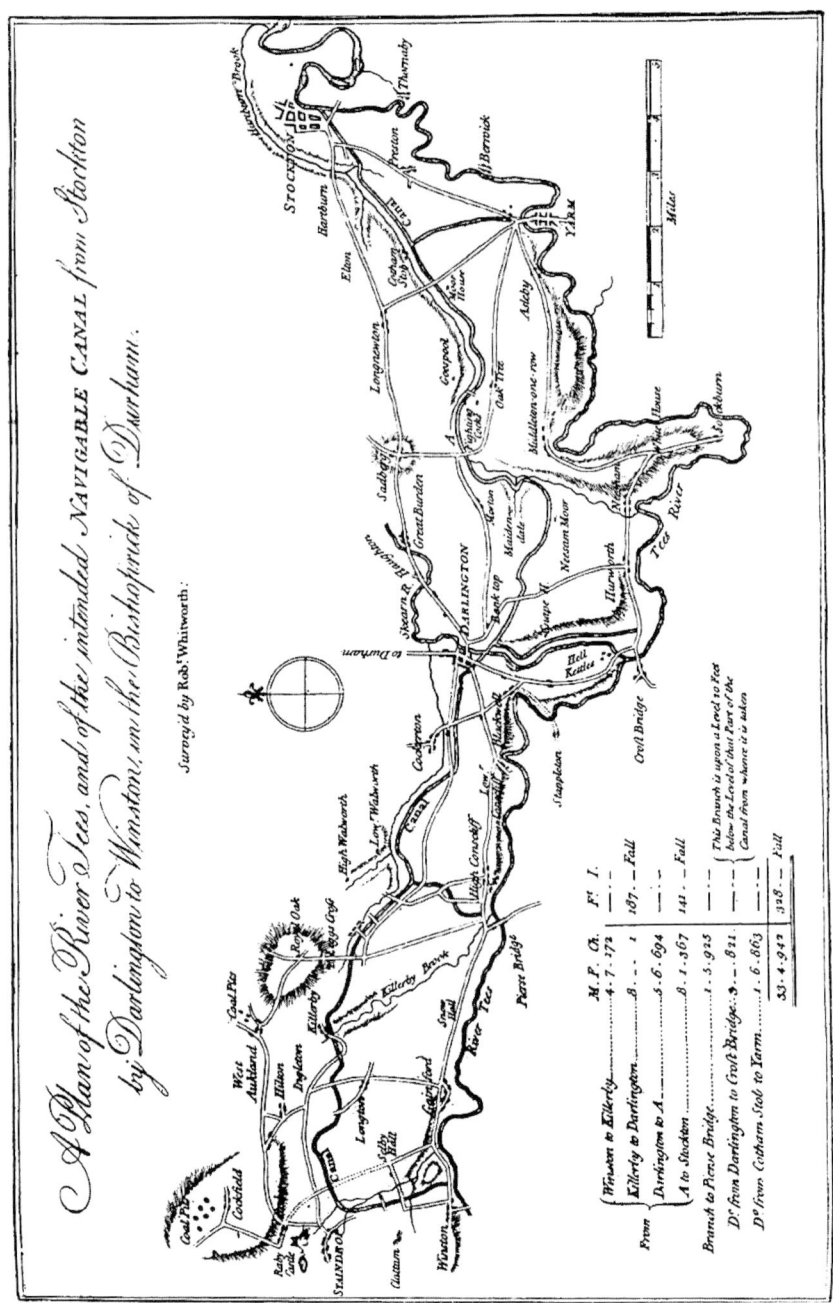

"On the arrival of the company in Croft, cheerings and congratulations of the multitude were most impressive," reported the Newcastle Courant. A celebratory luncheon – or, as the paper grandly put it, "an elegant dejeune a la fourchette" – was held at the Croft Spa Hotel.

"Mr (Francis) Mewburn, (the S&DR solicitor), who presided, actually made the startling prediction that in a few years a railway would be made from Darlington to London, travelling so quickly that the passengers could go up one day and come back the next, having witnessed a performance at Covent Garden Opera House in the meantime," said Edith Harper in her history of the village. "This prediction was greeted with loud laughter…"

Mr Mewburn was one of only a handful of far-sighted individuals dreaming of a railway network that could carry people from all over the country to take the waters of Croft. Nearly everyone else was just thinking of coal movements. Therefore, when Pilmore was placed on the market in 1829, Hurworth was a thriving, exciting, expanding place, its roads chock full of trains of pack-ponies bearing coal heading one way and men driving donkeys bearing linen the other way. And its air was full of the first smuts and the heady possibilities of the new age of steam railways. No wonder that the agents felt that the estate of Colonel Gordon Skelly was worthy of a purchaser from as far away as the monied metropolises of Newcastle and Leeds.

Yet when the hammer fell in the King's Head Inn – the main coaching inn in the centre of Darlington – shortly after 2pm on Monday, July 13, 1829, the purchaser turned out to be a neighbour, someone known to Colonel Skelly, someone already living inside the selfsame loop of the Tees as Pilmore, someone who would improve upon the colonel's handiwork and move the "most desirable mansion house and estate" further up the social scale.

Francis Mewburn

He was Thomas Surtees Raine, whose middle name proved his geneaology to the world: he was a member of the Surtees family which had made its name by owning land on the banks of the Tees – sur Tees. Indeed, the earliest Surtees had settled a couple of Tees loops downstream from Pilmore at Dinsdale in the 12th Century, from where the family had spread, accumulating power and land across Durham and Northumberland.

Yet Thomas was the third son of a second daughter, and the genepool didn't have enough properties for such an outer branch of the family tree to inherit anything, especially as his mother's eldest brother, Crosier, a "designing, artful man, a bad character", had married their cousin Jane. This spectacularly unhappy marriage had united the Surtees' Northumberland and south Durham estates but had left little to

The Road to Rockliffe

be left to others. So Thomas' mother, another Jane, had had to make her own way in the world. She married Joseph Raine, of Barnard Castle, in County Durham, and Batsford, a small Gloucestershire village in the Cotswolds.

They had at least three sons. The youngest, Thomas, also had to make his own way in the world (his elder brother William, for instance, seems to have had life sufficiently arranged for him to become the rector of Batsford), although there must have been some wealth trickling down the Surtees family tree to save him from penury.

What Thomas did with the first 50 years of his life – if, indeed, he did anything in the conventional working sense – is unknown, but on June 22, 1824, aged 49, he came home. He spent £2,790 buying two farms inside the Pilmore loop only four miles down that straight road from the Surtees' ancestral home of Dinsdale. He bought 52 acres ("be the same, more or less", says the deed) from the children of the recently deceased farmer, William Tinkler. These 52 acres were made up of the closes, or fields, known as Little Pilmore, Great Pilmore, Sunney Field, the Flat, High and Low Rospell, and High, Middle and Low Holme. "All which," says the deed, "are now known by the name of Hurworth Grange."

Thomas' land was to the west of the colonel's Pilmore estate. Today, it is the site of Middlesbrough FC's training complex. Although the Grange was probably the oldest settlement within the Pilmore loop, it was overshadowed by the colonel's property.

Still, though, it was an impressive purchase, because according to the deed it came "together with all and singular houses, outhouses, edifices, buildings, barns, stables, yards, gardens, orchards, backsides, church pews or seats, commons of pasture, common of turbary, trees, woods, underwoods, mounds, fences, hedges, ditches, ways, waters, watercourses, fishings, fisheries, liberties, privileges, easements, profits, commodities, emoluments, hereditaments and appurtenances whatsoever".

A turbary is a place where you dig turf or peat, but more interesting than that is the mention that Hurworth Grange came complete with ownership of a pew in All Saints' Church. This is further evidence that the Grange was originally the pre-eminent estate inside the loop (the poor old colonel in his Johnny-come-lately residence of Pilmore House didn't qualify for a pew).

Having taken ownership of the Grange, Thomas' next move was to find a wife. His

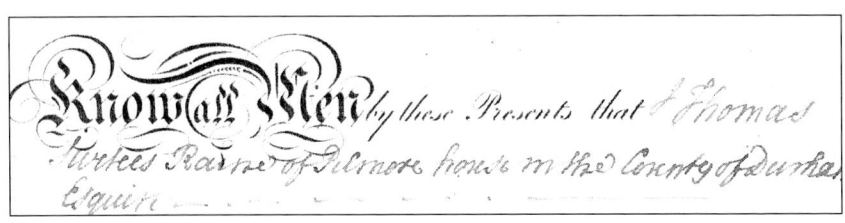

A fragment of an 1829 deed in which Thomas Surtees Raine buys the Pilmore loop

Weaving the Loop Together

eye alighted on Margaret Wallis, the daughter of the Reverend Richard Wallis, the rector of old Seaham, near Sunderland, and perpetual curate of St Hilda at South Shields. The vicar was a poet and a painter whose greatest claim to fame was that he had assisted at the notorious wedding of Lord Byron on January 2, 1815, at Seaham Hall – Byron's marriage to the heiress of the hall, his "princess of parallelograms", lasted only a brutal 12 months before he disappeared to die fighting for his hopeless, romantic cause in Greece.

The vicar had had four children, but his son had died young and his other two daughters were spinsters. Thomas married Margaret, who was many years his junior, at the Church of St Mary the Virgin in old Seaham on August 1, 1826. Nine months later, on May 5, 1827, the Reverend Wallis died, naming Thomas as the executor of his will.

Very sad. But very opportune. A further 18 months later, Thomas' neighbour, Colonel Skelly passed away, and when his Pilmore House went under the hammer on July 13, 1829, Thomas was a man of enough means to outbid whatever potential purchasers had come from Leeds to Newcastle. An idea of the price that he paid can be gained from the £5,000 "of lawful English money" that he borrowed on December 4, 1829, from three Northern notables: John Wilson, of Brigham, near Cockermouth, in Cumberland; Thomas Greenwell, of Greenwell Ford, near Lancester, in County

A painting, probably from the early 1830s and possibly by Thomas Surtees Raine. It shows the original Hurworth Grange where Thomas lived at that time. That may be Thomas, his wife Margaret and her sisters in the garden. Picture courtesy of Durham County Record Office D/x 332/69

23

The Road to Rockliffe

Durham, and Francis Mewburn, of Darlington, the famous railway solicitor who just five weeks earlier had stood up in the Croft Spa Hotel and predicted that within a few years, a person would be able to travel by railway from Darlington to London in a day. It was an accurate prediction – although Mr Mewburn didn't say that that railway would be within sight of the property on which Thomas had just spent £5,000.

The new year of 1830 dawned with Thomas Surtees Raine the undisputed master of the Pilmore loop. In five years, he had spent about £8,000 – £700,000 today according to the Bank of England's Inflation Calculator – joining the 52 acres ("be the same, more or less") of Hurworth Grange with the "170 acres or thereabouts" of Pilmore House for the first time since man had starting caring about such things as property ownership. And they would never again be rent asunder.

Thomas became an important man in the district. In 1831, he was "a steward" at the Hurworth Bazaar and Ball – one of the five local bigwigs who organised the charity event at the Croft Spa Hotel raising money to share between a new school "for female children" and the All Saints' organ. In 1836, he was sworn in as a Justice of the Peace.

So important was he that he was allowed to place his coat-of-arms on the Hurworth church in which he had a pew. He'd been granted his arms on December 1, 1814, and they are described as "ermine a pair of wings in lure (sable) on a canton (gules) an orle (gold) – Surtees-Raine". This description is meaningless unless you are either an expert in heraldry or you have access to a heraldic dictionary. Using the latter, one can build up a very rough translation: a pair of wings with their tips pointing downwards on a black background with a red corner division and a gold border.

Thomas Surtees Raine's coat of arms on Hurworth church

Most histories of the regularly rebuilt All Saints proudly point to the four shields "of great antiquity" on the western side of the belltower. These bear the arms of the ancient families of Neville, Tailboys, Dacre and Greystocks, and they are accompanied by a fifth which belongs to the Reverend Robert Hopper Williamson, the vicar who paid for the 1871 rebuild.

However, on the north wall of the transept (the north and south transepts are the arms of the church which create its cross shape) overlooking the road that runs straight as a die past Rockliffe, is another shield. It is overlooked and unmentioned by the other church histories, perhaps because it is so badly weathered. Nevertheless, one can still make out a pair of wings with their tips pointing downwards. Even the corner division, once red, can be made out at the top left.

As the Reverend Williamson was allowed to place his arms on the belltower when he paid for the 1871 rebuild, perhaps Thomas was similarly allowed to hoist his arms high when he contributed to the church's 1831 rebuild, which cost £1,965 16s 4d.

As well as his importance locally, the squire of Pilmore was becoming well-established within his mother's Surtees family. Their most respected member was her second cousin, Robert Surtees, the great antiquarian who lived at Mainsforth in County Durham. In his magnum opus, The History and Antiquities of the County Palatine of Durham, which was written at about the time his kinsman, Thomas, was buying property, Robert enthused that Hurworth was "a beautiful village scattered along a steep bank above the Tees, and commanding a rich though bounded landscape southwards, extending over a fertile plain, washed by a gallant sweep of the river; the swift rise of the Yorkshire grounds closes the prospect".

Robert died on February 11, 1834. His body was carried from Mainsforth for burial in Bishop Middleham churchyard on the shoulders of his grateful tenants. "The only ceremonial attendants," said the family's account of the proceedings, "were two mourners: Thomas Surtees Raine Esq of Pilmore Hall and Mr Ralph Robinson of Durham University." This was some honour for Thomas.

The Esquire after Thomas' name suggests that he was a man of independent wealth who had no need to soil his hands with toil, unlike the unfortunate Mr Robinson. It is said that Thomas was a landscape painter, but although his competence is undoubted, he appears to have been a hobbyist. Only two of his purported works are known to survive. One is said to show his wife Margaret and her sisters on the lawn outside what is probably Hurworth Grange (see Page 23); the other is an engraving which a London firm made in 1829 from his painting of Dinsdale. The engraving was widely reproduced for sale, so perhaps, given its date, Thomas might have been using his brush to fund the purchase of Pilmore. Alternatively, he may simply have been recording his family's homes – a case of now and then.

For a year, 1838-1839, Thomas lived in the Kingdom of Naples and he rented out Pilmore, but he was back home on July 18, 1845, when he died of "disease of the bladder" with the village doctor, Thomas Dixon Walker, at his Pilmore bedside. He was 69 and was buried in Seaham. Margaret outlived him by 25 years, first in the Grange and then in York, where she died in 1870. Because they had no children, control of the land in the loop passed to Thomas' cousin, Robert Surtees of Redworth Hall, to the north of Darlington. He had been the head of the family since the death of his philandering father, Crosier, in 1803. Crosier, "a mean and grasping man", had separated from his cousin-wife Jane after 31 years of cruel marriage and had gone to live in a remote cottage on the moors above Hamsterley with a local farm lass. He had met his end when, returning home one night very drunk from a banquet hosted by Lord Barnard in Raby Castle, his horse had failed to negotiate a moorland stream and he had slid from his saddle into the water. He was found next morning frozen to death. Surtees records say he was unlamented.

Under Crosier's son, Robert, in the late 1840s and early 1850s, Pilmore House and Hurworth Grange were let to gentlemen, but rarely for long. Advertisements stress

The Road to Rockliffe

that the properties were "within reach of the Raby Hounds and in the immediate neighbourhood of the Hurworth Hunt", so perhaps the gentlemen only rented for the season.

Or perhaps they found that during the time of Thomas Surtees Raine something big, noisy and steamy had been built on the western fringe of the loop, scaring foxes and deterring tenants of a rural inclination.

An engraving of Dinsdale from a painting by Thomas Surtees Raine in 1829. This is the only surviving work that is definitely by Thomas. Dinsdale is a few looping miles up-river from Rockliffe

4: The Age of the Train

ON November 2, 1836, Thomas Storey commenced work at Pilmore House, Hurworth. Storey was a Northumbrian mining engineer and a close acquaintance of George Stephenson who had brought him to work on the Stockton and Darlington Railway (S&DR) in 1821. Fifteen years later, Storey had risen to become the S&DR's chief engineer, and at Pilmore he started surveying the route for the proposed Great North of England Railway (GNE) which would link Newcastle, Darlington and York with Leeds and then London.

As early as 1826 – only a year after the opening of the S&DR – there had been talk of crossing the Tees and driving the railway to York. Joseph Pease, the south Durham MP and founder of Middlesbrough who controlled his family's industrial interests, had gained Parliamentary permission and set Storey to work.

The line was to be built in two phases – from Tyne to Tees (34½ miles) and then Tees to York (41¼ miles). To complete the 75¾ miles, Parliament was told that the railway company would need to raise £1,150,000 – a phenomenal amount, but this was the height of the railway-building phenomenon, and money was no object.

Originally, the Tyne to Tees section was to be first but, possibly because of Storey's survey which he completed in 14 days, it was decided to concentrate on the section to York. Durham was full of hills, rivers and rivals; the Vale of York was flat, level and uncontested by other companies.

On November 25, 1837, the GNE's chairman, George Hutton Wilkinson of Harperley Hall, in Weardale, ceremonially cut the first sod on the edge of the Pilmore estate and started the great railway enterprise. Life inside the loop would never be the same again.

There were four major obstacles on Storey's line to be overcome. At York, the River Ouse needed bridging. At Northallerton, Castle Hills, "a stupendous mound of earth" said to be "artificially formed" by the Romans, had to be dug through.

But it was at the Tees where the big problems lay. First of all, the river itself had to be bridged. Francis Mewburn, the railway solicitor, explained in his diary: "It will often be asked why so abrupt a curve is made at Croft. The reason is no other foundation could be got for the bridge than the one selected."

This one possible position meant that the river had to be crossed at an angle of 51 degrees, rather than at a conventional 90 degrees. Construction of this "skew bridge", therefore, was tricky. In March 1838, a contract worth £14,481 was awarded to Messrs Dees and Hogg of Tyneside to turn the designs of a Newcastle civil engineer, Henry Welch, into reality. "A stupendous bridge is now in the course of rapid erection," reported The Examiner newspaper on April 8, 1838. It was to be 471ft long and 58ft tall from the bed of the river to the top of the parapets, and its foundation stone was formally laid, reputedly on bags of sheep wool which was a common bridge-building method of the day, on May 8.

The second major problem that the Tees presented was its approaches. Two cuttings were required. One on the Durham side would enable the line to go beneath that long straight Rockliffe road. Croft station – Croft Spa station from 1896 – would sit within the cutting almost underneath the road bridge. Another cutting on the Yorkshire side needed 388,742 cubic yards of soil to be dug out to keep the line on the level around Dalton-on-Tees.

So as soon as Mr Wilkinson turned the first sod near Pilmore, the district was inundated with navvies and labourers. They came from every corner of the British Isles, but the Hurworth weavers were also well represented. Mechanisation was killing their trade and they could earn twice as much on the railway.

The village doctor, Thomas Dixon Walker, noticed a change in them immediately. "The consequence of men leaving a sedentary vocation for an active employment was followed by remarkable results," he wrote. "Those who escaped injury, earning good wages, and consequently living upon the fat of the land from being poor, and lean, unwashed artificers, swelled out into strong, muscular, powerful, and able-bodied men, so that in a few weeks I scarcely recognised them."

There are four key words in there: "Those who escaped injury." While the railway construction swelled the muscles of the lucky, it crushed the life out of the less fortunate. Dr Walker continued: "Many were killed or maimed through carelessness or want of proper precautions in forming excavations; others (like young solders who, when first under fire, see a cannon ball hopping along the ground, put out their foot to stay the missile, discover themselves suddenly a foot less), being equally

An Edwardian postcard view of Croft Spa station which was in a deep cutting

ignorant of any law of motion save that of the shuttle, in fastening waggons together whilst they were in rapid transit, thrust their heads between two waggons, and had their sculls fractured. The number of deaths from accident about half-a-mile on each side of the Croft station was fearful. Upon one occasion, three lay dead in our village on the same day."

He elaborated: "On July 23, 1838, I was called out of bed at 6am to attend an accident which had occurred in making the cut close to the present Croft station, and occasioned by the fall of many tons of earth upon the labourers. As rapid as I had been, upon my arrival I found that the labourers had been more expeditious, and had not only rescued the bodies – two in number – from the soil but had also, considering life defunct in each, laid them out in a coach house attached to the Comet Inn, at that time occupied by William Dawson.

"One poor fellow was dead, for his brains had been dashed out against the temporary rail, employed in the removal of the material. Whilst examining the other, who I was informed had been 12 minutes buried in the soil, I observed a slight motion in the upper eyelid of the right eye."

Being a proper medical man, Dr Walker added a footnote to explain the slight motion: "When death occurs in the human species, and perhaps also in the lower order of animals, the departure or extinction of life is almost invariably preceded by a spasm or trembling in the upper eyelid. There is a small nerve given off immediately from the brain, which, passing through the frontal bone, supplies the upper eyelid with the power of motion, and may be the means of causing this symptom or appearance, for the body is not always dead, even when it appears to be defunct."

With this thought uppermost, he continued: "I cleansed his mouth and nostrils from the soil, and with great difficulty poured some hot brandy and water down his throat, amidst the exclamations of those around that it was of no avail, for his body was wounded and he was dead.

"By means of a common quill I inflated his lungs. In a short time, he began to move his limbs. Reaction took place and in an hour-and-a-half I was able to take some blood from his arm. The injuries he had received were of a most distressing character as he had been tumbled topsy turvy upon his head, with an immense mass of metal between his thighs, separating them, and by its great weight and pressure lacerating his body most fearfully.

"In the evening of the same day he was able to sit up, and inform me that his name was McNichol, a muslin or calico glazer from Glasgow. He rapidly recovered."

Injury and death were not the only hazards. On October 20, 1838, the Leeds Mercury reported: "We are sorry to observe that riots amongst the men working on the railways are becoming common. Six or seven men working on the Great North of England Railway near Croft were indicted for this offence at the North Riding Sessions and were to be tried yesterday."

Three were imprisoned and three were fined, but they were the tip of the iceberg.

The Road to Rockliffe

An early drawing of a train travelling into Durham over the Tees Viaduct

So many others were imprisoned that soon Northallerton Gaol was overflowing "owing principally to the large influx of persons of loose and disorderly habits connected with the public works now being carried out in the district".

As the navvies came from all over Britain, they brought regional rivalries with them and lubricated them with ale. But there was more to it than just petty jealousies. On October 26, 1838, the Newcastle Courant carried a curious advert appealing for masons to work on the Tees Bridge. "Good workmen will meet with liberal encouragement," it said before claiming that the vacancies were "not on any account of any strike among the men now at the Bridge".

But they were. The riot coincided with the masons striking for higher wages, and principal contractor William Dees, on the orders of the railway company, sacking them all. However, the winter of discontent turned into the spring of 1839 and reports of industrial unrest faded from the papers. But progress remained terribly slow. For example, Mr Storey built 77 small bridges over little watercourses between Pilmore and York, but at 6pm on July 18, 1838, one of them – over a beck near Northallerton – had collapsed with no one near it. Then in early November 1839, a Scottish labourer found himself caught between two wagons near Thirsk "and his head was severed from his body, hanging only by the skin".

So there was probably great relief when on April 16, 1840, the keystone of the last of the four arches – the one on the Pilmore side – was cemented into place at noon by Mr Wilkinson who made a speech before adjourning to the Croft Spa Hotel for a celebratory four-hour "breakfast" in company of the Newcastle bridge theorist Peter Nicholson and his protégé, the designer Mr Welch, where they held a "discussion of the spiral principal on which the skew bridge was built".

Skew bridges were not new. Mr Storey had himself built one of the first in 1829 on the S&DR's Haggerleases branchline over the River Gaunless beside Cockfield Fell.

The Age of the Train

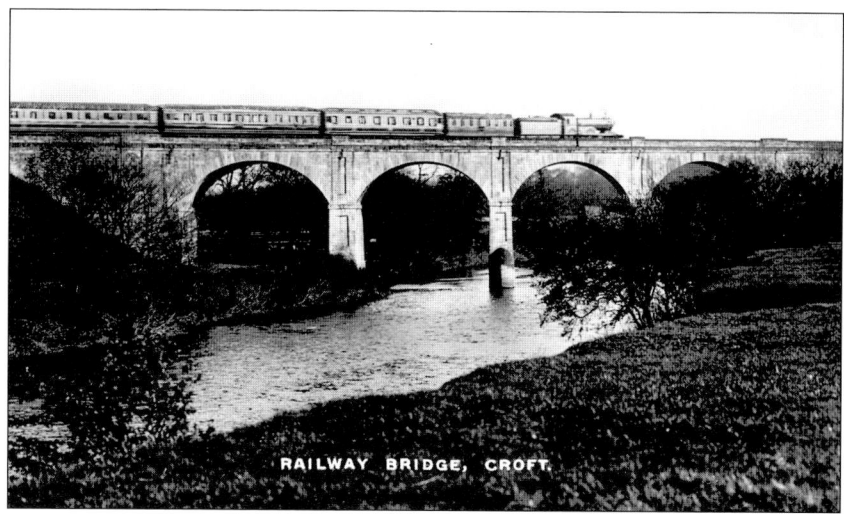

A postcard view of the Tees Viaduct, and, right, the plaque from the centre of the bridge. Alfred Backhouse paid the North Eastern Railway Company ten shillings a year to use the path beneath the bridge

They employed toilet roll technology: pull apart a toilet roll and you discover that its strength comes from it being one continuous spiral of cardboard. Stand beneath the Tees Bridge – or crawl beneath the Haggerleases skew bridge – and look up. The bricks are laid in a continuous spiral, like the cardboard in a toilet roll. When Mr Storey constructed the Haggerleases bridge, over the benign trickle of the Gaunless, the method was so green that they constructed a trial bridge of wood in an adjoining field to see if it really would stand up.

Ten years later, they were more confident, but the Tees Bridge – taking a mainline over a major river that enjoyed washing away man's puny constructions – was still one of the largest of its kind in the country. To commemorate its spanning, in the evening, after the midday four-hour long celebratory "breakfast", the workmen were invited to the Croft Spa Hotel for a meal. They presented James Hogg with an

31

The Road to Rockliffe

inscribed silver snuff-box "as a token of admiration of his abilities and of respect for him as a master".

Yet in many ways they were celebrating too soon. Work was now at a standstill because it wasn't until June that the timber arrived for the top. Frustrated, the company set an opening date for November 25, 1840, but it wasn't until December that the rails arrived. To make up for lost time, the workmen had to labour on Christmas Day.

And on January 1, 1841, resident engineer at the bridge Thomas Ridley wrote in his diary: "I rose this morning at quarter past two o'clock and got some ballast...to help fill up the Way. I spread it with my own hands. At five o'clock, three engines all attached to 64 wagons of coals came along while I stood alone on the bridge and viewed the train by the light of the moon which had now nearly sunk below the horizon, and you may believe I felt great joy at seeing it pass safely along."

Three hours later, another three engines with 101 heavily laden wagons passed over, "followed by another exactly similar". Mr Ridley completed his entry: "These immense trains would extend for a length of 350 yards. The Tees Bridge never complained."

On January 4, 1841, the bridge was ceremonially opened to mineral traffic. Two of the S&DR's locomotives – Pilot and Witton Castle from Darlington to York, and Magnet and Tory on the homeward leg – pulled trains of 99 wagons and carriages on the inaugural journey over the Tees Bridge. In one wagon was a single lump of coal

An Edwardian postcard view showing the Tees Viaduct at Croft-on-Tees

weighing over a ton – an advertising gimmick boasting to the world about the size and quality of the Durham seam.

There were scenes of great rejoicing all along the line as the 44¼ miles were covered at an average speed of 15mph – this discounted an enforced two-hour delay near Thirsk as another of Mr Storey's bridges over the line had collapsed onto the tracks smothering them with debris.

Joseph Pease missed the train back to Darlington but, as the line was his brainchild, a special train carried him home at a rattling lick of 26mph.

Yet the GNE was in a mess. It "appears to have been, at the outset, one of the worst-managed undertakings in the kingdom, and that is saying a great deal", said the Railway Times. The company had spent all of its £1.15million and yet was only halfway through its plans to connect Newcastle with York. Another company, the Newcastle and Darlington Junction Railway (N&DJR), would have to be formed to complete the northern half.

The opening day debacle near Thirsk was the last straw for Mr Storey. He took the blame for all the delays, caused by riot, strike or bridge collapse, and was compelled to resign. Robert Stephenson was appointed engineer-in-chief to finesse away his failings.

For all that, the line has proved a success. Today, the straight and flat section of the line through the Vale of York is still one of the fastest on the East Coast Mainline, and, of course, with the engine and carriages mingling with the treetops, a train crossing the lofty Tees Bridge it is still a mighty impressive sight as it speeds along the western boundary of the Rockliffe estate before disappearing into the cutting where so many navvies had lost their lives.

The N&DJR finally opened on June 18, 1844, allowing a passenger to travel the length of England by rail – from Gateshead over the Tees Bridge, into London and out the other side to Southampton.

Exactly 13 months later, within sight of the grand viaduct, Thomas Surtees Raine died in Pilmore Hall. Who would want to take ownership of his beautiful loop now its peace was shattered by the puffs and sobs of the steam engines?

Only a man who was steeped in railways, who would use railway money to buy the exquisite estate and who would lavish an enormous fortune constructing a parkland with views that showed off the majesty and power of the new mainline to the full.

5: Introducing Mr Backhouse

IN 1819, on Croft Bridge, just down the road from Rockliffe, a member of the Backhouse family dramatically saved the fledgling Stockton and Darlington Railway from a devious, dastardly plan concocted by a duke. In doing so, he spawned one of the worst puns in local history. For the Backhouses, it was as if this joke broke the ice and started a relationship that would last 90 years and would have a profound impact on the land within the looping Tees.

Backhouse money was crucial in getting the S&DR going in 1825 and in funding the railway's continued expansion so that, in 1840, the Tees Bridge could carry the new mainline along the boundary of the Pilmore estate. In return, the railways and their related industries re-paid the Backhouses so profitably that by the 1850s, the head of the family could afford to buy the entire estate with its artful, industrial backdrop that his father's investment had helped to create.

The Backhouse story begins in 1746 when James Backhouse (1721-1798) came over the Pennines from his native Lancashire in search of love. He was from a family of Quaker flax-dressers, and the thread he followed led him to Darlington where fellow Quaker Jane Hedley, three years older than he at 28, was the sole heiress of her father's linen fortune.

Textiles were in those days largely manufactured by piece-workers, like the Hurworth weavers, in their own homes. The washers would wash and pass the washed product on to the bleachers who would bleach and pass the bleached product on to the spinners who would spin and pass the spun product on to the weavers who would…and so on. Chalonweavers, fullers, silkweavers, jerseycombers and hecklemakers all played their part in the chain.

But as the century grew old, steam-powered machines revolutionised the working practices, forcing all the little cottage industrialists under one roof in a giant mill where they became the employees of an entrepreneur who had the vision, the bravery, the contacts, the technical know-how and the wherewithal to raise the money to buy the machines.

James had all of these qualities. In 1790, he purchased a Boulton and Watt steam engine, and his mill on the Skerne, opposite St Cuthbert's Church, became the first in Darlington to be steam-powered.

James also had another quality: trustworthiness. People were prepared to give him their money and gold, trusting him to bank it for them on his travels to London – he went regularly in both business and Quaker capacities. In return, he would issue a reliable receipt. The banks in London came to trust him, too, and soon he was able to issue bills on their behalf. Almost by accident, he became a banker, and so, in 1774, he opened his own bank with his eldest son, Jonathan (1747-1826).

That same year, Jonathan married Ann, the daughter of Edward Pease (1711-

1785) who was the major Quaker linen entrepreneur in Darlington. Edward was creating a mill bigger than the Backhouses' a few hundred yards upstream on the Skerne.

United by marriage, the co-religionists didn't compete directly with one another. The Peases became the front men running the mills while the Backhouses became the backroom bankers, raising the capital that the Peases required to run those mills.

Having liased in many different ways in the late 18th Century, these two families came to run Darlington and the Tees Valley in every conceivable way for nearly all the 19th Century. When that century dawned, they were already out-growing the textile industry. Indeed, the second Edward Pease (1767-1858) had made so much money making army uniforms during the Napoleonic War that when peace was declared in 1815, he was contemplating retirement – not bad for a 48-year-old pacifist Quaker.

But three generations of the two families had listened to plans first hatched in 1767 to link the coalfield of south Durham with the sea at Stockton so that the black gold ripped out of the bowels of the earth near Bishop Auckland could be lucratively transported to the London market. In 1812, in the era of canalmania, that third generation had the money to make such a move.

The second Edward Pease and the second Jonathan Backhouse (1779-1842) paid for John Rennie – the king of the canals – to devise a £205,618 watery link from Staindrop through north Darlington and onto Stockton.

The nationwide banking collapse of 1815 sank their canal plan. The crisis was so deep that only the Backhouses' trustworthiness kept them afloat – on Black Monday, they awoke to find that their most influential customers had plastered Darlington town centre with posters protesting their utmost confidence in their bank.

Jonathan Backhouse (1747-1826), the founder of the family bank who was the grandfather of Alfred, the creator of Rockliffe

With so much entrusted in them, the Backhouses emerged from the crisis stronger – and more pre-eminent – than before. Their rivals, Mowbray, Hollingsworth and Company, had gone under leaving Backhouses the only bank in town and a substantial empty premises on High Row. Backhouses took on Mowbray's customers and moved into its prominent bank, and then despatched Edward Backhouse (1781-1860) – younger brother of the second Jonathan – to set up a branch in the vacuum Mowbray had left in Durham City.

Nowhere did the banking crisis hit harder than Sunderland where both the Shields Bank and the Wear Bank folded. Bereft of bankers, it was on the brink of total

35

The Road to Rockliffe

The original Backhouses' Bank, on the left of the picture, on High Row

collapse. "Names of the highest respectability were involved in the financial ruin, owners of mansions, shipyards, shops and factories were sold to the door," wrote Sunderland historian GW Bain in 1905. "The tension of the times set up a degree of lawlessness unexampled in our local history, and house and highway robbery was rampant. As banks could not be trusted, money was kept at home, or carried on the person, and frequent attempts were made to get at it."

A delegation of Sunderland businessmen approached the Darlington Backhouses desperate for a branch in their town to save them from the lawlessness. Edward answered their call, and for 13 years he was the only banker in Sunderland. It would be the making of him, and it would have a profound impact upon Pilmore.

As the economy emerged from its post-Napoleonic Wars slump, Backhouses found themselves with 16 branches beyond Darlington (Durham and Sunderland plus Askrigg, Bedale, Barnard Castle, Bishop Auckland, Easingwold, Guisborough, Northallerton, Reeth, Richmond, Kirkbymoorside, Staindrop, Stockton, Thirsk and Yarm). Soon a third brother, William (1779-1844), was despatched from Darlington to set up a branch in Newcastle.

In July 1818, the economic revival encouraged a contingent of Stockton businessmen to revisit the idea of connecting their town with the coalfield by canal, bypassing Darlington. When Jonathan heard, he rapidly revived his pre-crash consortium and a strange race developed between Stockton and Darlington to see which would be the first to gain Parliamentary permission for its transport link.

Introducing Mr Backhouse

Far left: Jonathan Backhouse (1779-1842) who "balanced the cash". Left: His brother Edward (1781-1860) who was the father of Alfred, the creator of Rockliffe

Darlington won. Stockton's businessmen couldn't prove to Parliament they could raise the £200,000 needed to dig their canal and so they crashed out of the race at Christmas 1818.

Darlington won because it had the Backhouse brothers. Darlington needed £120,900 to show Parliament that its scheme was viable. Between them, Jonathan, William and Edward Backhouse contributed £21,000 and Jonathan's wife's family – the Gurneys of Norwich, also Quaker bankers – subscribed a further £20,000. Most of the rest of the money was rustled up by the Backhouses from the Quaker community across the country. The Peases' contribution was only £6,200, although Edward Pease would be the driving force and the figurehead who become known as "The Father of the Railways".

Then another race, far more dramatic, began. The transport link had evolved from a canal into some form of steam tramway – no one was really sure yet what form it would take, but they knew it would be land-based rather than floating on water.

When Lord Cleveland, the Earl of Darlington who lived in Raby Castle at Staindrop, heard he immediately took against the Quaker Railway. His lordship lived for his fox-hunting and feared that if such a thing – possibly hauled by noisy, belching steam engines – were to rattle across his land, the foxes would be too scared to come out to be chased. So he set out to block the railway Bill in the House of Lords while he devised a cunning plan closer to home to derail it forever.

In those days you could, on demand, have your £1 banknote exchanged by your bankers for a pound of gold. His lordship planned to quietly accumulate a vast quantity of Backhouse notes and then, unannounced, descend on the bank in High Row and demand there and then that they all be converted into gold. The Backhouses, of course, would not have enough gold in their vaults. They would be forced to either withdraw their £41,000 from the railway, or they would go bust.

The Road to Rockliffe

Either way, the railway would die due to lack of funds. No doubt cackling evily, his lordship ordered all his tenants – and as he owned all Teesdale and much of Darlington, there were plenty of them – to collect Backhouse notes.

But in July 1819, Jonathan got wind of the devious scheme. He immediately drove by day and by night down the Great North Road to London where he went round his Quaker banker friends drumming up a war-chest of gold bullion. Then he dashed the 225 miles homewards, fearing that the duke's agent, laden with notes, was about to darken the bank's doorstep at any moment and destroy the railway dream. By the fourth day, Jonathan was nearly home. He'd reached Croft Bridge, four miles from safety – and liquidity.

Crash! As he crossed the bridge over the Tees, one of the four wheels came off his carriage. He couldn't continue. Yet a fearful vision of the duke's agent closing in on High Row drove him on.

Thinking fast, he shoved the bullion off the damaged front axle, and piled it up at the rear the carriage. This caused the front to rise up and, with three wheels on his wagon, Jonathan careered into Darlington, and took his place behind his desk, waiting for the agent to arrive.

When he did, Jonathan calmly converted all the notes into gold as requested, and added disdainfully: "Now, tell thy master that if he will sell Raby, I will pay for it with the same metal."

Jonathan's action of moving the gold from the broken front axle to the stable back one so that the carriage regained its equilibrium is known in local history circles as "how Jonathan Backhouse balanced the cash". It is an appalling pun. But it is a true story. The Backhouse accounts read: "1819, 6th month, 25th. To Bank and Cash to London, £32,000." Followed by: "1819, 7th month, 31st. £2 3s – wheel demolished."

How Jonathan Backhouse balanced the cash in 1819 on Croft Bridge

38

And so, for an outlay of two pounds and three shillings, the railway was saved. The S&DR opened on September 27, 1825, and rapidly expanded: on October 27, 1829, for example, the branchline opened into Croft, within spitting difference of the bridge where the railway had been saved.

From 1823 to 1832, the S&DR's share price rose from £80 to £315. The Backhouses prospered. The railway's success emboldened them to use their monopoly and to invest more of their bank's money into similarly risky new industrial ventures.

For example, Edward, the only banker in Sunderland, allowed the Hetton Coal Company to have an overdraft of £107,000 in 1822 and the following year he advanced it a further £80,000 – even though the company was headed by the failed banker Arthur Mowbray. It quickly paid dividends: by 1830, Hetton was making a profit of £50,000-a-year and its annual banking charges were £1,309. Edward had so many other similar clients – he loaned the Marquis of Londonderry £50,000 in the mid-1820s to exploit his east Durham coal reserves – that by 1830, aged 49, he was able to convert his branch into a Joint Stock Bank and then, in 1836, retire on the vast profits.

He moved out of the town centre terrace called Sunniside, which was only a minute or so walking distance from the bank, and built a marvellous mansion, Ashburne, on the fashionable country fringe to the south-east. Ashburne was a brisk walk from the beach, protected from the sea winds by belts of trees. It had a dramatically elevated position overlooking the deep Valley of Love through which ran the Ash Burn – one of Sunderland's two principal brooks. Here, Edward

Ashburne in Sunderland, the childhood home of Alfred, the creator of Rockliffe
Picture courtesy of Durham County Record Office D/Wa 3/6/2

indulged his passion for plants, creating a glorious pleasureground of specimen trees, multi-coloured carpet-bedding and exotic shrubs and succulents which Quaker missionaries had collected around the world. A huge conservatory protected the more vulnerable items; vast glasshouses in the kitchen gardens brought on poinsettias, orchids, peach trees, pelargoniums, fuchsias and begonias, as well as vines and figs. Bridges criss-crossed the babbling brook, a graceful fountain captured the eye, an elaborate octagonal summerhouse provided shelter should the weather turn.

"At the bottom of the incline we take a turn to the left, and the beauty of the place is spread before the eye in all its loveliness," said The Journal of Horticulture.

Edward died at Ashburne in 1860. Sunderland University now occupies his mansion; Backhouse Park takes up his pleasureground. "He was a generous-hearted man who contributed liberally to many of our local charities," said his obituary in the Sunderland Herald. "He was one of the earliest and most influential promoters of the Infirmary."

He had five children. His two daughters married comfortably; his three sons were set for life.

The eldest, another Edward (1808-1879), inherited Ashburne and could afford to give away £10,000-a-year to charities. He enjoyed yachting in Norway and sketching in Switzerland. He was a pioneer photographer. He wrote a book about early church history. He built up such a large collection of zoological, botanical, archaeological and ethnographic items that a new wing had to be added to Ashburne to house them all. In his will in 1879, he left £180,000 – at least £17 million in today's prices, and didn't do a single day's paid work in his life!

Edward Backhouse (1808-1879), elder brother of Alfred, the creator of Rockliffe

The second son was Thomas James (1810-1857). He pre-deceased his father by three years, and as his wife had already died three years earlier, he left three orphan boys aged 15, 12 and four.

And the third son was Alfred (1822-1888). Unlike his elder brother, Alfred served in the family bank and amassed a greater fortune – in his will he left £369,911 1s 1d which is worth at least £37 million today. A very private man, the centrepiece of his life and fortune was his sumptuous country estate tucked away within an extravagant wind of the Tees and flanked by the railway that had helped make him.

6: The Botanical Backhouses

ALFRED BACKHOUSE'S beginnings were totally urban. He was born on September 28, 1822, in a large terraced house in the centre of Sunderland into a family that had made its fortune out of heavy – and often filthy – industry. But it was a family that liked to breathe. It was a family of botanists. It was a family of large parks and wild open spaces, of great trees and delicate blooms. A family that found God's perfection in Nature but which still managed to make it that little bit better through skilled human intervention.

Quakers made good botanists. One theory is that their strict, puritanical religion forbade so many things that other people found enjoyable – drinking, dancing, singing, joking, having a good time – that all that was left to fill their waking hours was a long walk in the countryside. Another, more charitable, theory would say that these were highly intelligent men who, having amassed fortunes through their clever endeavours, had the money to indulge their passion for the fashionable pursuit of horticultural excellence. In their century, the world was starting to shrink. Year after year, as Great Britain's soldiers and explorers pushed deeper and deeper into uncharted territories, new and exotic specimens were being sent home to beautify the hothouses of the rich so that their neighbours bloomed red with envy.

Alfred's mother, Mary Robson, was a scion of one of the finest botanical families in the North-East. His great-great-uncle Stephen Robson (1741-1779) produced Hortus Siccus, a collection of nearly 600 dried flowers found in the Darlington district and arranged in families with their names written for the first time in common English – previously botanists had stuck to unwieldy, scientific Latin names.

Alfred's maternal grandfather, Edward Robson (1763-1813), created a collection entitled Plantae variores agro dunelmensi indigenae – Rare plants native to Durham – which is now in Sunderland museum. In his work, he identified the Downy Currant which grows only in the North-East, a discovery so great that shortly after his death he had a North American gooseberry named Robsonia in his honour (as everybody knows, the gooseberry is of the same family as the redcurrant).

The botanical interest on the other side of Alfred's family tree started – perhaps by accident – with his paternal grandfather, Jonathan Backhouse (1747-1826), the co-founder of the bank. In the early 19th Century, Jonathan bought vast tracts of open moorland and poor quality grassland in Weardale. The purchases might have been spurred by a love of Nature in its bleak, moory glory, or they might have been a shrewd investment. Industry was consuming vast quantities of timber, turning it into pit-props for the local lead and coal mines and into ships in the yards from Tyne to Tees.

Jonathan's three sons went to work in Weardale, probably spurred on by the Royal

Alfred Backhouse (1822-1888), the creator of Rockliffe

Society of Arts. From 1758 to 1846, it awarded medals to those who planted trees on land unsuitable for agriculture. This was to stimulate the timber supply in times of war, to encourage employment of the rural poor, and to "ornament the nation".

The eldest of the three sons was Alfred's uncle Jonathan (1779-1842). In 1813, he won a Silver Medal for planting 271,000 larches at Shull, near Hamsterley – an area Alfred would come to know very well. In 1825, Jonathan became the first of the newly-prosperous Quakers to buy a country estate – Polam Hall, in Darlington, now a school – and dabble in ornamental horticulture. He laid out its 36 acres, which sloped gently down to the River Skerne, with gardens and shrubberies, and dug a large fishpond as a centrepiece. These tentative trowel-markings inspired his kinsmen, but the opulence so horrified his wife, Hannah, that in 1830 she went as a Quaker missionary to America for five years, enduring great hardship while spreading the word of God.

The second eldest was William (1779-1844), another uncle to Alfred. In 1813, he won a Gold Medal for planting 300,000 larches and 50,000 other timber trees at the top of Weardale. In 1825, when he was despatched to Newcastle to found a branch of the bank, he became a founder member of the Natural History Society of Northumberland, Durham and Newcastle-upon-Tyne. He married the daughter of a mollusc specialist and became a grass and moss expert, although in his Darlington estate of Elmfield, he specialised in herbaceous borders and alpine rockeries. Elmfield upped the landscaping stakes with a boating lake and a romantically-ruined folly of a boathouse, plus it boasted only the second mulberry tree in town. North Lodge Park now occupies most of its grounds and the tree is beneath Mulberry Street. William's son, William, bred 192 types of daffodil in Weardale, including the giant Weardale Perfection, and his grandson, Robert, stunned the botanical world with one of the great bulb breakthroughs of the 20th Century: the pink daffodil, which he named after his late wife, Mrs RO Backhouse.

The third eldest was Alfred's father, Edward (1781-1860). In 1814, Edward won a Gold Medal for out-planting his brothers: 363,000 larches and 67,000 timber trees at St John's in Weardale. Edward didn't just plonk saplings into the peat and hope for the best. His was the "side of a rugged hill with a north-facing aspect", according to horticulture historian Peter Davis. "In his application (for the medal, Edward) noted that larches did not thrive in wet, boggy areas. He overcame this difficulty by making open drains or, where this was impracticable, he planted alder, birch and willow."

From the late 1830s, as we've seen, Edward turned the Valley of Love in Sunderland into his personal pleasureground, which is now Backhouse Park. Alfred spent his late teenage years there, watching the planting of the new pines and firs that are only now reaching their peak. Alfred's elder brother, Edward (1808-1879), inherited Ashburne and continued with the hothouses. But this Edward was also an artist, and he illustrated the work of the greatest botanical Backhouse of them all: cousin James (1794-1869).

Cousin James was born in Darlington but suffered so terribly from asthma that he spent months convalescing in the pure air of Teesdale. He fell in love with the dale's unique Alpine flora which triggered his lifelong love of botany. For the sake of his chest, he required an outdoor profession. He trained as a nurseryman, but as no suitable business were available in Darlington, in 1815 he and his brother Thomas (1792-1845) bought a long-established nursery in York.

In the 1830s, James combined his love of botany with a Quaker missionary zeal and sailed to Australia. He introduced the Society of Friends to the colony and kept meticulous records of the strange plants he found growing Down Under, sending back seeds to brother Thomas running the nursery in York. After six years, he turned for home, coming back via Mauritius and South Africa. He recorded his findings in two books, published in 1843 and 1844, which were illustrated by Edward's engravings. In honour of his knowledge and achievements, a small family of aromatic evergreen shrubs which grow in the rainforests of eastern Australia was named after him: the Backhousia.

James and his son, also James (1825-1890), built up their nursery until it covered 100 acres – a greater area than Kew Gardens. It had 40 glasshouses, an underground fernery and a £2,000 towering rock garden (about £190,000 in today's money) made from 1,500 tons of rock. Alpine plants clung to the rocky cliff. In the 1840s, James and James travelled from York to Teesdale for plant-collecting expeditions so regularly that the room in which they stayed at the High Force Hotel is still known as Mr Backhouse's Room.

Given the closeness of the Backhouse family, given that brother Edward illustrated cousin James' books and stocked his own extraordinary country retreat near Hexham from the York nursery, given that the nursery was the first in the country to sell the Californian tree that would become Alfred's trademark, given that in Alfred's properties there are two Alpine rockeries of the kind that James specialised in, given that the nurseryman would have regularly travelled by train along the very edge of Alfred's splendid estate on his way to Teesdale, given that the nursery was at its peak from 1860 to 1890 just as Alfred inherited the money to lavish on his pleasuregrounds, it is inconceivable that the two cousins – Alfred and James – did not work on the Pilmore project together.

Pilmore was destined to be Alfred's crowning glory. Almost from the moment he was born in the centre of urban Sunderland, you can feel his desire to follow his family and immerse himself in the beauties of botany.

After being taught at home, he began his banking career in the Durham branch – Sunderland was out of the question as family rules forbade a son learning under his father. By his mid to late twenties, he was established in a senior role in the Darlington headquarters and secure enough to buy the Greenbank estate. This had been the home of his maternal grandfather, Edward "the Gooseberry" Robson, where his mother had grown up, although it had been out of the family's hands for a couple of decades and it was nothing like it had been in their day. The town was swallowing it up, building terraces across its fringes.

In 1848, at a Quaker wedding, Alfred met the bridesmaid and triggered a classic Quaker love affair. She was Rachel Barclay, of Essex. Her mother was a Gurney from the Norwich Quaker bank and her father had headed Barclay, Bevan and Company, of Lombard Street, a London Quaker bank. With their family trees already intertwined, Rachel made a perfect wife for a Backhouse banker, and they married on May 8, 1851, in Plaistow, Essex.

"On Thursday evening last, upwards of one hundred workmen, who have been employed in the alterations and repairs of the Greenbank residence of Alfred Backhouse Esq. sat down to a repast provided for them, at that gentleman's expense, at the Sun Inn," reported the Darlington and Stockton Times of May 10, 1851. The

The Botanical Backhouses

Sun Inn in Prospect Place (where Midland and HSBC banks have been since the 1920s, looking at Joseph Pease's statue) was then Darlington's premiere hostelry.

But Greenbank's five bays and three storeys, created by upwards of 100 workmen, were soon not enough for the happy couple. Their eyes alighted on the land within a loop of the Tees at Hurworth where Nature in all her glory was bounded by the engineering magnificence on which Alfred's fortune was based. Since the death of Thomas Surtees Raine in 1845, the mansion had been rented out by Robert Surtees, of Redworth, to a string of wealthy figures such as David Laird, who followed the district's blood sports. Early in 1857, Robert agreed to rent Pilmore to Alfred but before the sealing wax could be applied to the deed, Robert died. After an understandable delay, Robert's son and heir, Robert Lambton Surtees, signed the lease on May 25, 1857.

It states that Alfred had to insure Pilmore for £2,000-a-year (about £170,000 today), maintain the mansion and paint the exterior in "good and proper oil colors" once every four years. He was not allowed to plough fields nor cut down trees, but he could build "hothouses, pits and conservatories" and "plant any ornamental trees or shrubs he may think fit".

And there were specific instructions on how Alfred had to maintain the pleasuregrounds. He had to "keep the garden and garden ground lawn and shrubberies belonging to the said mansion house well cropped and manured and managed the same according to approved methods of gardening and that he will not cut down or destroy any of the fruit trees, shrubs or any other trees or shrubs now growing …(except such trees as shall be decayed or shall cease to be productive of fruit)…but will carefully preserve the same trees and shrubs and cause the said fruit trees to be properly pruned at seasonable times of the year, and that he will plant in the place and stead of every fruit tree which shall be decayed or become unproductive during the said term and which shall be cut down by him or them a thriving tree of proper growth of the same sort of fruit…".

Rachel Backhouse (1826-1898), Alfred's wife

Alfred was in. But only as a tenant. And he had to put up with a Captain Cookson renting the neighbouring Hurworth Grange.

Still, it was enough for him to begin to see the possibilities and potentials of Pilmore. He bought all the land in the loop outright in 1860 – surely no coincidence that his father died on June 7 that year and Alfred inherited a third of the estate of one of Sunderland's richest men. Then he set to work in Hurworth.

7: *Project Pilmore*

AT 2.30pm on Wednesday, December 9, 1863, the floor of Darlington's new Covered Market gave way, plummeting nearly a dozen perplexed men and three extremely large prize cattle 12ft into the cellar beneath. Builders had been working for two years on the market complex, and although it wasn't yet complete, its brickwork was still "green" and its iconic clocktower had barely reached headheight, the Northern Counties Fat Cattle and Poultry Society was holding its prestigious annual show inside.

The collapse happened on the show's second day, less than an hour after "shilling time", or reduced admission, had been declared.

"At two o'clock the place was literally swarming, and the difficulty of moving about was felt by all, especially by the ladies, whose wide skirts increased the difficulty tenfold," said the Darlington and Stockton Times (D&ST). The paper's reporter pushed through the crowd and pressed the flesh of the prize-winning bull. "We dipped our fingers into the soft, velvet sides of the prize ox and had just turned from it . . . when a sudden crash fell on our ears, and immediately before us, not more than three yards off, we perceived a wide chasm, and a number of men at the very brink transfixed for the moment with terror, and not knowing which way to turn."

Getting its priorities right, the D&ST reported that the cattle – Nos 27, 28, and 29 in the show catalogue – were unharmed.

But as to the humans: "There appeared to us eight or ten men writhing with pain and struggling to rise out of the midst of rubbish in which they so suddenly found themselves engulfed."

The most seriously injured was "Mr Robert Robson, 55, farmer of Newton Morrell (near Barton village, five miles west of Rockliffe), whose face was a shy pale, and whose leg appeared to dangle loosely as he was being carried out of the hole". His broken right thigh bone could be seen protruding through his skin, so Dr William Haslewood tied his legs together with towels and put him in a cab, which bounced him over the cobbles to a relative's house in Northgate. There, having rallied enough to make a will and resign himself to his fate, he died two days later.

It was a disaster for many people beside the unfortunate Mr Robson. It was a hideous PR gaffe for the 18 members of the Local Board of Health. The board, the forerunner of the local council, was chaired by William Backhouse, of Elmfield, Darlington, and St John's, Weardale, and included his 41-year-old cousin, Alfred Backhouse of Pilmore. It had commissioned the market despite local opposition which deplored the encroachment onto the traditional open Market Place and which accused the board of self-aggrandisement. The market complex was also to include a town hall in which the board would meet.

An Illustrated London News drawing of Darlington's Covered Market in 1864

Then there was the controversy regarding the appointment of the architect. In 1860, the board had held an open competition to find the best design, but not one of the entries from local architects had been deemed good enough, and so it had appointed a little known 31-year-old from Manchester, Alfred Waterhouse (1830-1905). Waterhouse had just scored a major triumph with the Manchester Assize Courts – a splendid conglomeration of towers, turrets and arches – and was seeking to spread his wings over the Pennines by doing little embellishments on Backhouse properties in the Blackwell area of Darlington. Like the majority of board members, Waterhouse was a Quaker, and, again like many board members, was related to the Backhouses by marriage: his wife of less than a year just happened to be the stepdaughter of another of Alfred and William's cousins.

The condemnation of Quaker nepotism was loud but proved, over time, to be

The Road to Rockliffe

misplaced. Waterhouse was not a dodgy draughtsman. He would become an architectural artist who would be hailed as the greatest Gothic practitioner of his day in the entire country, producing several of the greatest buildings of the Victorian era, notably the Natural History Museum in South Kensington, London, and Manchester Town Hall. Plus, of course, Pilmore Hall in Hurworth.

Even so, the fatal collapse of the Market Hall floor was a far from auspicious start. "The cause of the accident is attributed to the adoption by the architect, Mr Waterhouse of Manchester, of flat arches," wrote Francis Mewburn, the Peases' railway solicitor, in his diary. "Robson, the leader of masonry work in Darlington, on inspecting the plans declined to offer a tender for the masonry work, as he was satisfied the building would not stand."

The inquest into the unfortunate farmer – not from the same family of Robsons as the masonry leader – was not attended by the architect which caused raised eyebrows. The eyebrows rose higher when it was revealed that the clerk of works, Samuel Harrison, had tested only one of the six cast iron girders that held up the floor.

Mr Harrison said each girder was designed to support 35 tons and yet one had snapped with only 12 tons of man and beef standing on it. "It was a perfect mystery to me," he said. A succession of local experts explained the mystery by claiming that the architect had not taken into account the stresses of a moving load. They alleged that Waterhouse's girders could not have held more than eight to 15 tons of wandering bull and milling crowd. The jury concluded: "We are of opinion that Robert Robson came to his death from injuries received by the . . . breaking of a metal girder which in our opinion, founded upon the evidence given, was not of sufficient strength to bear the weight placed upon it."

This was potentially devastating for the fledgling architect. But the inquest had also heard that when the girder snapped, it revealed a flaw in its middle. It was suggested that when the girder was

Alfred Waterhouse, the architect of Rockliffe, and, above, Manchester Town Hall

48

fashioned at a nearby foundry, a piece of ash had been accidentally rolled into it, making it fundamentally but undetectably weaker.

The architect's friends rallied round. A trial of strength was held at the scene of the disaster. "A number of scientific gentlemen", including Thomas Bouch, builder of the ill-fated Tay Bridge, and Alfred Kitching, founder of the Whessoe foundry, gathered in the market to test Waterhouse's workmanship.

The Darlington Telegraph reported: "One of the trial girders broke by a pressure of 26 tons on the centre, the other bent a little at that pressure, this showing that the section made by the architect was correct and that the unfortunate accident was caused by a flaw in the casting," reported the Darlington Telegraph.

Waterhouse was exonerated. But just to be on the safe side, a further £2,000 was spent providing extra support for the market floor and Waterhouse never again built solely in iron. His reputation was undimmed – certainly in the minds of the Darlington Quakers, who were watching with approval his second major project in the district: the complete rebuilding of Pilmore Hall.

Months after work on the Market Hall began, Colonel Gordon Skelly's old country home within the loop of the Tees had been razed to the ground. On top of its cellars, a Waterhousian wonder grew: a symphony of chimneys, a drama of rooflines, a bounty of bays, a collage of windows, a brilliance of balustrades, and a cunning contrast of stone and brick. These were topped off by a wealth of detail, a multitude of pinnacles, finials, weathervanes and even a minaret – ideas that had been stolen from financial institutions, appropriated from cathedrals and nicked from chateaux across Europe and throughout time.

It took two phases and two decades. The first phase was from 1861-4, cost £14,335, and was the east wing. The second phase was from 1873-9, cost £15,000 and included the long west wing plus a complete recreation of the south elevation and a delicate reshaping of the east frontage to make it baronial yet ecclesiastical at the same time.

By the end, Pilmore was two mansions in one reflecting the two sides of its owner's character. Visitors arriving from the north were greeted by an immense frontage of solid proportions in stern red brick with few irrelevant details – the merest hint of a hidden arch here and a touch of detail on the roofline there. If, as they entered through the sturdy square porch, they wondered who would live in a house like this, the architecture answered. Someone big and strong who was unshakeably reliable and had little time for the risky or the frivolous: a great banker.

Yet, round the rear, a different character emerged, one full of originality, individuality and fun. Initially, Pilmore faced as much east as south so that it looked over Thomas Surtees Raine's established pleasureground towards the misty outline of the Cleveland Hills. The east elevation is still the most remarkable architectural juxtaposition: a powerful Victorian bay next to a giant Norman cathedral window which is flanked by turret from a Scottish baron's castle.

But as Alfred developed the agricultural land to the south, he re-orientated his hall. In the late 1870s, he erased the southern elevation, including a second Scottish

The Road to Rockliffe

The first phase of Pilmore, built between 1860 and 1864 looking east with only a small south-facing conservatory.
Picture courtesy of Durham County Record Office D/Wa 3/6/2

baron's turret, and filled it with picture windows and light-catching bays so that the house looked southwards. He even added his own version of the Backhouse coat-of-arms in the stonework by the conservatory – a very unQuakerish adornment.

The interior was also full of Waterhousian features. Waterhouse designed the chimney breasts plus his own furniture, colour schemes and finishing touches. "Do you wish my purpose-made bar fenders supplied for your tiled hearths?" he asked Alfred in a letter. Certainly by the time of the second phase, he had mastered the art of the ornate ceiling, arranging simple plaster ribs in a variety of interlocking shapes.

The interior would have been put together by Victorian Britain's best craftsmen who worked closely with Waterhouse. The heating apparatus was made by Haden, of Trowbridge. Stone carving was by Farmer & Brindley, the great architectural sculptors and ornamentalists of the day whose carvings, like icing on the top of the cake, graced all of Waterhouse's best buildings. The stained glass was by Heaton, Butler and Bayne, of Covent Garden, who had a worldwide reputation and were known as "stained glass masters".

And all the decoration was by Best & Lea who were much more than mere painters and decorators. Charles James Lea was an artist in his own right, painting the ceilings and plaster panels of the National History Museum with beautiful trees, butterflies, fruits and flowers.

Curiously, then, the contractor on the first phase was Edward Robson, "the leader of masonry" who only months earlier had refused to work on the Market because he feared the architect's flat arches would cause it to fall down.

We can only imagine how the construction of the first phase unfolded. The early 1860s were bedeviled by strikes in the district, the Covered Market being held up first by a dispute among the masons – one of the youngest masons was accused of doing too much work so they all downed tools and demanded a rise from 27-shillings-a-week to 30 – and then another involving the joiners.

Pilmore probably suffered similarly. It certainly did during the second phase. The Northern Echo was founded in 1870 and its small ads reveal how the 1875-77 phase unfolded. An advertisement appeared on November 26, 1875. "Masons wanted," it said. "Apply to the foreman at Pilmore Hall."

From February 10, 1876, a second advert started appearing daily: "Wanted: about 20 Good Masons. Wages 34s per week." From March 2 onwards, the words "No Strike" were appended to the ad, which seems a strange protestation.

Then the advert of March 7 read: "Notice – Masons are requested to keep away during the dispute from Pilmore." So, despite the protestation, there was a strike.

A resolution was in sight by the end of the month. March 31's advert said: "To Masons – The C.C. having declared the Strike at Pilmore Hall ILLEGAL the Job is now open." (The C.C. was presumably the County Court where industrial disputes were heard.) But April 6 contained the message: "To Masons – The C.C. have NOT declared the Strike at Pilmore Hall illegal and we hope Masons will take no further notice of false statements."

The Road to Rockliffe

Project Pilmore

> **NOTICE.—MASONS** are requested to keep away, during the dispute, from Pilmore, Hurworth. 99
>
> **TO MASONS.**—The C. C. having declared the Strike at Pilmore Hall ILLEGAL, the Job is now open. 313
>
> **TO MASONS.**—The C.C. have NOT declared the Strike at Pilmore Hall illegal, and we hope Masons will take no further notice of false statements. 410

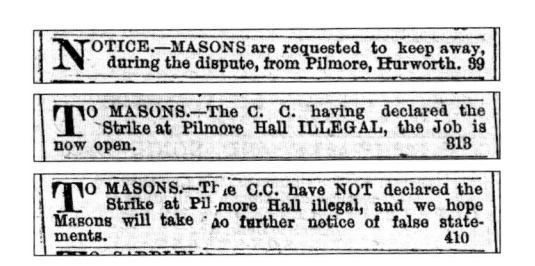

The curious adverts from The Northern Echo's Business Notices of March and April 1876 suggesting there were industrial relations difficulties

Opposite page: at work on the second phase of Pilmore in 1876

This was followed on August 2 by what can only have been a spoof advert. "To Masons – Wanted Several BANKER HANDS; also one FIXER – Apply on the Works, Pilmore Hall." In the trade, a fixer or "fixing mason" was someone employed as the project neared its end to skilfully fix the little snags, but from this it sounds as if work on the great banker's mansion had been becalmed during a summer of strife and he required a skilful conciliator to get his men back on board. One wonders to what strike-breaking subterfuge Alfred had resorted if he had provoked someone to publicly make this point at his expense.

A fixer was found and the works got going again. Later in August, Pilmore advertised for "3 or 4 good bricklayers at once", followed in September by "3 or 4 good Carpenters; also one Mason for Fixing". By 1877, the construction was all but complete. In March, the adverts, still hinting at industrial unrest, said: "To Plasterers – 12 good men WANTED at once at Pilmore Hall. No strike." By mid-April, there was a call for three or four Stone Wallers, and at the end of the month there was a call for Painters: "Wanted 6 good BRUSH HANDS at once." By the end of the summer of 1877, Pilmore faded out of the Echo's small ads. The job was obviously done; the banker was in his splendid castle.

Yet, there could have been a third phase. Waterhouse was instructed to design a clocktower for Pilmore in the late 1870s. As well as Darlington's iconic clock tower which came as part of the market complex, such opulent statements became a feature of Waterhouse's country houses and he had just completed one at Pierremont, "the Buckingham Palace of the North", which was the home of Henry Pease. Pierremont was even more sumptuous than Pilmore; its grounds so fantastic that they were opened to the public in 1870, and visited in six years by 10,000 people from far and wide. Pierremont's clocktower was its crowning glory, peering grandly over the roofline, its delicate chimes telling visitors of the creeping of time as they marvelled at the Italian gardens and the Swiss chalet or crossed the ornamental bridge over the serpentine lake.

There must have been some rivalry between the Peases and the Backhouses, Pierremont versus Pilmore, even if it was only friendly. Therefore, Alfred might have wanted a clocktower if only for the sake of keeping up with the Peases. Indeed, we can speculate that it had always been part of his grand design to bring his west wing to a dramatic end with a tower. There is a vacancy for such a full-stop in the south-

The Road to Rockliffe

west corner. From there, the clock would have peered imperiously over the roofline, clearly visible to all the visitors as they came down the long, straight drive, and its sonorous chimes would have been heard throughout the land within the large loop of the Tees.

Sadly, it never came to pass.

Alfred Waterhouse's splendid Pierremont, built for Henry Pease at the same time as Pilmore, only complete with clocktower: is this what Alfred Backhouse wanted?

Alfred Waterhouse's specifications for Contract No 100
Pilmore Hall, Hurworth

New coachmen's cottages, alterations and additions to house amounting to rebuilding, new stables, extensions to hall, 1861-4. Further alterations and extensions 1873, 1875 (proposed alterations and tower set aside 1877-9).
Contractors for both: General W Richardson & Co; Thomas Robson (1861-4); J Parnell & Sons (1876-9). Heating and ventilation, GN Haden, DO Boyd. Stone carving, Farmer & Brindley. Tiles, T Oakden; Taylor; WB Simson & Son. Stained glass, Lavers & Barraud; RB Edmundson; Heaton Butler & Bayne. Chimney-pieces, W Wilson; J&H Patteson; Joseph Bonehill; Hopton Wood Stone Co; WH Burke. Decoration, Best & Lea. Furniture and fittings, Henry Capel. Ironwork, FA Skidmore, R Jones; W. MacFarlane; Hart Son Peard & Co. Bells, Warner & Sons.
Clerk of works: GG Hoskins
1861-4: £14,335; 1876-9: £15,000

8: The Great Darlington Frog

WATERHOUSE couldn't work alone. He was in demand all over the country. While the first phase of Pilmore was under way, he was finishing off the Manchester Assize Courts, a practical yet daring building which "astonished England". Then he started Strangeways Gaol while setting up a practice in New Cavendish Street, London. As Pilmore's second phase began, Waterhouse was putting the finishing touches to Manchester Town Hall, a classic of its age, and he was embroiled in the detail of his masterwork, the Natural History Museum. In addition, he was in the middle of rebuilding Eaton Hall in Cheshire for the Duke of Westminster, the richest aristocrat in the land and the rebuild was probably the most expensive country house project ever in England. The two phases of Pilmore cost only £30,000 (about £2.6m today); the museum cost a mere £412,000 (£36m); Eaton Hall cost a staggering £600,000 (£52m).

When it was finished, Nikolaus Pevsner, the renowned architectural critic, described it as "an outstanding expression of High Victorian originality. This Wagnerian palace was the most ambitious instance of Gothic Revival domestic architecture anywhere in the country, and to approach the front . . . was an unforgettably dramatic experience". It even had its own clocktower, which bore a striking resemblance to Big Ben at the Palace of Westminster in London. Whenever the Duke approached his house, the bells chimed out There is No Place like Home. How our Alfred must have sighed with envy!

With so many demands on Waterhouse's time, he needed someone to act as his eyes and ears in Darlington where, despite the embarrassment of the collapsing market, Alfred Backhouse had entrusted him with two major projects: Pilmore Hall (1861-4, £14,335) and Backhouses Bank in High Row (1864-7, £12,185).

GG Hoskins

Waterhouse sent George Gordon Hoskins (1837-1911) north to be his clerk of works, thus introducing to the Tees Valley an architect who would have a profound impact on its character and whose "Hoskinian Gothic" style would cause Darlington to become known as "the Athens of the north".

To understand GG Hoskins' fevered Gothic imagination, we have to go back to his

55

The Road to Rockliffe

great-grandfather, Abraham, a solicitor who, in 1795, celebrated his appointment as High Bailiff of Burton-on-Trent, in Derbyshire, by building Newton Hall, an elaborate Italianate mansion. In the parkland, GG's grandfather – another Abraham – built a fashionable but frivolous folly on the top of Bladon Hill overlooking the River Trent. Designed by Sir Jeffry Wyatville, the leading Gothic architect of the day, it was a wall topped with turrets, castellations, battlements and pointy, castley windows. From a distance it looked like a great castle commanding the heights, dominating the landscape.

But the Napoleonic Wars were at their peak. England could be invaded at any moment. The nation was so jittery that in Hartlepool a monkey was hanged as a French spy. The Hoskinses' neighbours in Burton and Newton Soley were less gullible, but were still greatly disturbed by the bellicose frippery that had come to adorn their hilltop.

Such was their outcry that the Hoskinses hurriedly added some habitable rooms behind the wall, and quickly moved into "Bladon Castle", as if their plan all along had been to live in it. Unfortunately, there was no water in the castle. Daily, a donkey had to haul supplies up the hill. The folly was by now wildly over budget and with Abraham Jnr lavishing money on his greyhounds, in 1836 the family was forced to sell the estate – mansion and "Hoskins' folly" – to their neighbour, Lord Chesterfield, and move to a more modest abode.

And so, on October 28, 1837, in Birmingham, GG was born. Despite the family's decline in fortune, there was an air of prosperity, and his godmother was the Duchess of Gordon. After he was well-educated in London and Paris, the Duchess wanted him to enter the church, but as he was showing an artistic bent, she assisted with his architectural studies. He joined a practice in Westminster and, in 1863, aged 26, linked up with Waterhouse. Waterhouse sent him to Hurworth.

Soon there were tensions between clerk and architect. Waterhouse, as well as being a brilliant artist, was a very efficient businessman. He prided himself on being economical and on his budgets being watertight. He insisted on frequent reports

The Great Darlington Frog

from his clerks – perhaps because he'd had his fingers burned by the market clerk who hadn't been on top of things – and on forensic scrutiny of contractors' accounts.

Hoskins, whose ancestors had frittered away a fortune, was in those early years at Pilmore not so meticulous. During the first phase, the chief clerk of Waterhouse's Manchester office wrote an exasperated letter to the architect in London in which he was very rude about young Hoskins. He wrote: "I enclose a letter from the Great Darlington Frog and hope it will enable you to take the whole case before Mr Backhouse, unless indeed you think it better the said frog should collapse (like his illustrious ancestor) by the very violence of his own conceit."

Waterhouse riveted the Frog to proper operational procedures and the working relationship was soon on a better hopping. In fact, Hoskins liked the project so much than when his son was born in Hurworth, he named him Harry Pilmore Hoskins.

While overseeing Pilmore, 26-year-old GG won his first solo contract: the £650 Temperance Hall at the east end of the village. Joseph Pease laid the foundation stone and Alfred Backhouse performed the opening on December 27, 1864. "The architect who designed a building of so much beauty that could be erected for so small sum must be possessed of as much ingenuity as taste, and we heartily congratulate Mr Hoskins on the success of his work," said the Darlington Telegraph.

GG was made. He had an "in" with the district's wealthiest people, and he was developing his own style. Alfred commissioned him to build banks in Barnard Castle, Middlesbrough, West Hartlepool and Sunderland, and he won his first educational contract in 1872, for Darlington's Queen Elizabeth Grammar School. When it was finished in 1878, locals didn't know what to make of it. It conformed to no known architectural style. It had a tower, arches, numerous rooflines and open cloisters so that it out-Waterhoused Waterhouse. But because of Hoskins' background, it also had a feeling of fading opulence and a mock Gothic grandeur that he borrowed from the castellated hilltop silhouette of the folly that had ruined his grandfather. So they christened it "Hoskinian Gothic", which is as good a label as any.

Even as his own practice thrived, Hoskins kept abreast of developments during

Right: The first example of "Hoskinian Gothic": the Queen Elizabeth Grammar School in Darlington which is now the town's Sixth Form College

Left: Snowy Pilmore in the 1870s (DRO D/Wa 3/6/2)

The Road to Rockliffe

Top: The Gamekeeper's Cottage at Pilmore which is either by Waterhouse or Hoskins.
Centre: Middlesbrough Town Hall, which was Hoskins' biggest contract.
Left: Darlington library of 1884-1885, another example of "Hoskinian Gothic"

Pilmore's second phase. For instance, on May 17, 1873, he placed an advertisement in The Northern Echo informing any builder interested in tendering for "the erection and finishing of four cottages at Pilmore for Alfred Backhouse Esq" that they "may inspect the Drawings, Specifications and Conditions of Contract at my Offices in Northgate".

Waterhouse usually designed the lodges for his estates, with elaborate barge boards around the roof and deep porches kept up by turned timber supports, as has the Gamekeeper's Cottage on the Pilmore estate. However, he was also content for a local architect to adapt his designs to suit the site. Despite getting off on the wrong lily pad, he clearly rated Hoskins, allowing him to design in 1867 the bank manager's house and stables behind the magnificent Backhouses Bank on High Row. Perhaps the Great Darlington Frog was responsible for Pilmore's outhouses, of which only the Gamekeeper's Cottage remains, and even for the stables which are now romantically ruined in front of the hotel spa. In fact, Waterhouse regarded Hoskins so highly that when he was invited to judge the 1877 competition to design Middlesbrough Town Hall, he awarded GG the £300 first prize ahead of the ten other entries, and then gave him some advice on how to make it even better.

How GG's heart must have swelled with pride when, amid great pomp and ceremony, the £130,000 town hall was opened on January 23, 1889, by the Prince and Princess of Wales, the future King Edward VII and Queen Alexandra. It is a grand building, full of gates and towers and great touches. GG had acquired the nickname of "Pitch Pine Hoskins" because many municipal contracts required him to use cheaper materials on the inside. Middlesbrough, though, got a sweeping stairway, an assembly room with ecclesiastical windows through which the light floods dramatically, and an imperious council chamber.

In short, newborn Middlesbrough got a town hall that declared to the world that it had come of age, although the ravages of time have caused the green Westmoreland roofslates to turn black and the pale stone to weather. It still looks terribly imposing, but now there's a touch of Gothic foreboding about it. Plus, modern shopping centres and court complexes have encroached around it, so that it flounders a little like a fish out of water.

So perhaps to find the best example of Hoskinian Gothic, we have to return to Darlington where, during his 40-year career, he created the town's architectural character. He covered his buildings in a mock-horror fantasy of belltowers, gable urns, overpowering entrances and sky-scraping classical statues. You can imagine the sky turning black behind any one of them, the lightning flashing overhead, a dark crow cawing ominously in a belltower and the cloaked shadow of Dracula sweeping out of the crypt.

The King's Head Hotel was a little different. Until the great fire of August 2008, it had the drama of Hoskins' other works, but also a touch of elegance and opulence. There is a grandeur to the "four spacious and elegant bay windows" of the first floor, and a glamour to the balconettes and the balustrades as the eye rises higher. When

The Road to Rockliffe

Hoskins' finest: the King's Head Hotel, Darlington

it opened on June 1, 1893, local newspapers called it "palatial" and "a temple of luxury". Even in its fire-damaged state, it is worth staring at. In its day, it must have been mind-blowing, with a regal front door – protected from the weather by a glass and cast iron canopy – in the middle of Prebend Row. Inside was all marble mosaic flooring, polished walnut panelling and sparkling mirrors. A sumptuous staircase led up to the lofty, handsome ballroom – although many visitors must never have made it that far, overcome by an apoplexy of delight brought on by the ground floor toilets.

"Even the general lavatory is a marvel of complete fitting, being fitted up with solid royal rouge marble, the walls lined with glazed tiles, and fitted with massive mirrors, and the whole equipment being in the perfection of sanitary work," enthused the Northern Review.

Ill health overtook GG after he had begun the initial drawings for Darlington's new theatre. He retired in 1907, handing his practice over to his brother, Walter, and died in 1911. "He has distinguished himself by his great architectural genius, abundant evidence of which is manifest in his imposing buildings," said the mayor of the day. "He has left many things behind him to keep his memory fresh."

And it all began for the Great Darlington Frog at Pilmore.

9: Woodland Beauties

OF COURSE, there's more to Rockliffe than just the Waterhousian wonder of a banker's mansion. And there's more to Alfred Backhouse than just banking and building a Waterhousian wonder. "Mr Backhouse was an ardent horticulturist and an enthusiastic admirer of Nature," said his obituary in the Darlington and Stockton Times of September 8, 1888. "His residence at Pilmore is famous for its woodland beauties, and the cunning of its arrangement. The deceased gentleman was never so happy as when he was roaming about his grounds, noting their yearly growth and planning improvement for the future."

Colonel George Skelly started laying out the pleasure ground; Thomas Surtees Raine took it on, refining the formal garden to the east of the hall and creating parkland all around – the oak and yew saplings that he planted are now glorious and mature, such as the eye-grabbing thicket in the middle of the golfcourse.

Then came Alfred. In 20 concentrated years, from 1860 to 1880, he built upon the best of what had been planted before and created one of the finest parklands in the north of England. At its centre was his mansion, set like a diamond in a ring, a jewel in a crown.

How much of this is the product of the brain and brawn of Alfred alone is open to conjecture. Architect Alfred Waterhouse was renowned as a one-stop shop, designing mansions complete with their estate surroundings: the out-buildings, the lodges, the stables, the walls, the balustrades, the fences and the whole landscape. So our Alfred could have taken advice from him.

Then there was big brother Edward, 14 years his senior. Edward's Sunderland mansion was in the park that their father had laid out, and he was planting up a hugely ambitious country estate at Dukes House, near Hexham, with his wife, Katharine. Alfred and his Rachel visited Dukes regularly, and Edward recorded in his diary the trees that they planted. So Alfred could have taken advice from him.

Then there was cousin James in York who ran one of the foremost nurseries in the country, scouring the world for specialities to sell. Alfred almost certainly bought from him and, as this was an extremely close family, it is highly likely that he was visited by him. So Alfred could have taken advice from him.

And then in the west end of Darlington was Henry Pease's Pierremont, drawing visitors from far and wide to view its horticultural magnificence with another Waterhousian backdrop. Although Henry was 20 years older than Alfred, the two families were tied tightly together in business and politics – both national and local – and the two men prayed together in the Friends Meeting House in Skinnergate. So Alfred could have taken advice from him.

But the obituary suggests that these "woodland beauties" were the grand passion

The Road to Rockliffe

of only one man with an equally grand vision. So let's imagine a visitor in a horse-drawn carriage in 1880 bumping along the road to Rockliffe. He arrived at the top of the drive, drawn in by a low, welcoming, curving wall behind which was a small, half-timbered lodge house. Then he clip-clopped towards the great banker's front door with Mr Backhouse's vision unfolding before him.

Biding farewell to the lodge house, the visitor entered the dark wood that Alfred planted around 1860 with ornamental trees – horse chestnut, lime, beech, oak, elm – and shrubs: rhododendrons, laurels and yews.

Originally the drive was straight, but Alfred snaked it so that the visitor emerged from the darkness of the wood into the light of a vast parkland. The centrepiece of this first view was a one-acre lake, but because Alfred wanted to create an impression of enormity with a buildingless vista, the little boathouse was hidden by a small clump of strategically planted oaks.

A screen of tall trees behind the lake forced the eye to pan southwards, mirroring the movement of the carriage. Suddenly – to gasps of astonishment – there was a break in the trees and through it the distant but dramatic outline of the Cleveland Hills.

As the carriage swung round to head due south, the next view was another screen of trees, guarding the mansion from sight. The visitor could only imagine what was behind the theatrical curtain, creating a delight of anticipation in the carriage. Little did the visitor know that to the east, the screen hid the paraphernalia of the walled garden – the

The Pilmore lodge house in the snow. (Picture: DRO D/Wa 3/6/2)

gardener's cottage, the potting sheds, the tall brickwork of the heated double wall with its cast-iron fireplaces and smokeboxes – and to the west it concealed the stables.

To break up the screen, Alfred cleverly planted clumps of oaks in front of it. As a Quaker, he liked his oaks. There are 450 species of oak, but only two are indigenous English. They are the shipbuilding oaks: the peduncular (acorns on long stalks) and the sessile (stalkless cups). Alfred had both.

He preferred, though, Turkey oaks. Recently arrived from Asia, they were planted for their sturdy good looks. Their timber, though, was poor, and they were nicknamed the "wainscot oaks" as they were only suitable for interior panelling.

Alfred also had a few Lucombe Oaks, with fluffy, mossy acorn cupules and slender leaves that the tree retains over winter. It was named after William Lucombe, an Exeter nurseryman, who crossed a cork oak with a Turkey oak in 1762 and created a tree with timber that he liked so much that he kept planks of it underneath his bed ready for the coffin in which he would sleep for eternity. He lived to be 102.

Alfred appears also to have had a rare Hungarian Oak, whose acorns can be ground to make coffee, and a Red Oak, which he imported from North America. This singular specimen stands beside the entrance to today's Clubhouse, by the golf course, where its rich red autumnal colour can, in a good year, be quite devastating.

While contemplating the oaks, the visitor's eyes would naturally be traversing the screen from east to west. As they reached the western end, there was another opening out that should have produced more gasps of astonishment, because, through the impressive outlines of a Scots Pine and a Cedar, could be seen the graceful but towering arches of the Tees Viaduct. It was breathtakingly picturesque in its own right but it was also distant enough for the stench of the railway not to take the visitor's breath away. The lucky visitor might even have been treated to the sight of a steam train passing over the bridge, a plume of brilliant white smoke trailing behind it, a contrast to the beautiful blue sky and a reminder – perhaps even a celebration – of the source of Alfred's wealth.

The carriage on the drive began to dip on its final approach to the hall. The magnificence of the building was still guarded by the screen of trees, but had Alfred completed his project, the clocktower would have been enticingly visible in the centre of the drive, magnetically drawing the visitor in.

As the screen neared, the visitor would realise that it was a fashionable pinetum, featuring pines and conifers from North America and Asia. These trees had only begun arriving in Britain in the 1860s when Alfred started his project.

Woven into the screen were four specimens of sequoiadendron "wellingtonia" giganteum – the largest living organism on the planet. Although well known to native Americans, British explorers had first discovered the trees in California in 1833. Despite their immense height, the British had then somehow lost sight of them until they were rediscovered in the Sierra Nevada Mountains in 1852. William Lobb, a British botanist, collected samples and seeds the following summer and dashed back to Exeter with them. On his arrival on December 15, 1853, the tree was named "wellingtonia" after the Duke of Wellington – the greatest of war heroes who towered over all other humans – and one of his first specimens was planted by the second Duchess of Wellington – the late duke's daughter-in-law – at the family home of Stratfield Saye House, between Reading, in Berkshire, and Basingstoke, in Hampshire.

American botanists were aghast. How dare the British appropriate a tree that had nothing to do with them and name it after a bellicose fellow for whom the Americans did not care! This was botanical imperialism at its worst. So perhaps it is safer to

The Road to Rockliffe

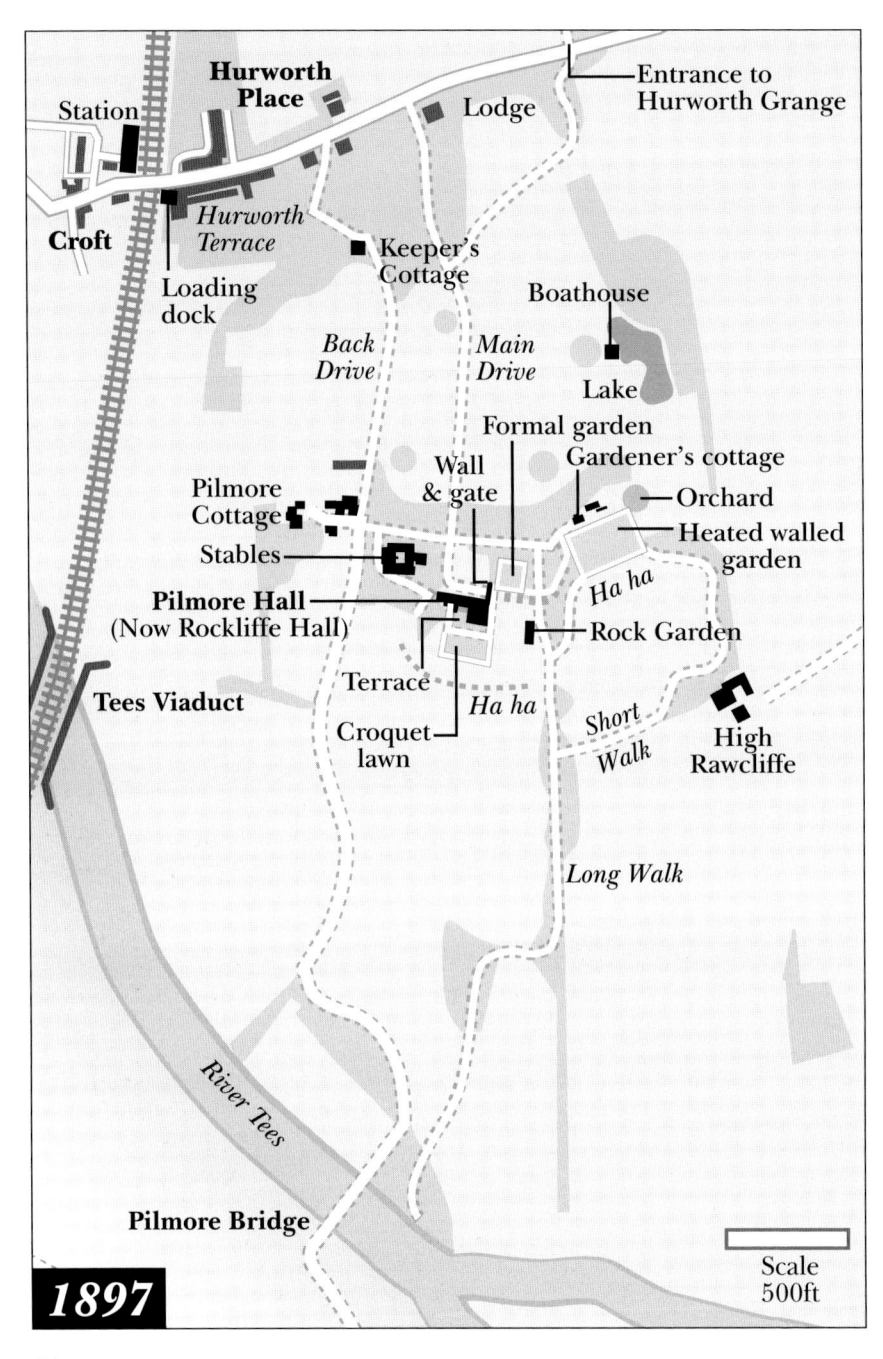

Map labels:

- Station
- Hurworth Place
- Lodge
- Entrance to Hurworth Grange
- Croft
- Hurworth Terrace
- Keeper's Cottage
- Loading dock
- Boathouse
- Back Drive
- Main Drive
- Lake
- Formal garden
- Gardener's cottage
- Pilmore Cottage
- Wall & gate
- Orchard
- Heated walled garden
- Stables
- Ha ha
- **Pilmore Hall** (Now Rockliffe Hall)
- Rock Garden
- Tees Viaduct
- Terrace
- Ha ha
- Short Walk
- High Rawcliffe
- Croquet lawn
- Long Walk
- River Tees
- **Pilmore Bridge**
- Scale 500ft

1897

refer to the tree as a sequoiadendron. But this name was given to it by a trouble-making French botanist, Joseph Decaisne, in 1854. He saw the political difficulties of wellingtonia and so cheekily proposed an alternative. Now British botanists were aghast! How dare a Frenchman name a tree which had been discovered by the mighty British Empire. Such impudence!

So perhaps it is safest to refer to it by its nickname: the giant redwood.

Nurseryman James Backhouse started selling one foot high giant redwood saplings in 1858 for a guinea each. Edward Backhouse was an early customer for his estate at Dukes House, closely followed by younger brother Alfred for Hurworth. In fact, Alfred liked the giant redwood so much that on March 11, 1863, he gave two specimens to Darlington's South Park to celebrate the wedding of His Royal Highness Albert Edward, the Prince of Wales (later Edward VII) and Princess Alexandra of Denmark. These sequoias are now among the park's finest talking points as in 2007 the British Tree Council placed them in the Top 10 of great British trees. Most giant redwoods bolt straight up to the sun – the tallest is 94 metres (308ft) – but the sapling the second duchess had planted at Stratfield Saye House in 1853 had sprouted many stems with boughs growing down to the floor before they curled round and heading sunwards. The only other sequoias in Britain known to perform such a feat are the pair Alfred gave to South Park, so it is believed that they, like that of the duchess, are from the very first batch of 1853 redwoods.

The Pilmore sequoia grew straight and true in the pinetum screen. Far-flung specimens east and west marked the outer limits of the property, and another pair stood sentry-like on either side of the drive, guiding the visitor in and perhaps – in Alfred's mind's eye – framing the clocktower he never built.

Only today is the pinetum truly serving the purpose for which Alfred planted it. Now the trunks of the pines and the redwoods are tall, slender and bare of lower branches and leaves. As the visitor approaches, he gets tantalizing views of the complex filtering through the trunks, allowing him to gradually build up a mental picture of what lies ahead.

Finally, the visitor pushes through the curtain, and at last the hall – and today the whole hotel and spa complex – is laid before him. But his carriage is so close, he hasn't time to take it all in. He's just left with an overwhelming impression of the enormity of it all.

Alfred's Victorian visitor would have swung round to the east, the wheels on his carriage crunching to a halt on the gravel outside the main door. Instead of going straight inside, he may have been tempted to see more woodland beauties and, with Alfred pushing open the heavy, wrought iron gate, he would have stepped into the east garden hidden behind the screen wall.

To the left, was a square formal garden, with immaculately trimmed box hedges, specimen flowering shrubs and paths of brightly coloured gravel. Further on were the heated walled gardens and the orchards, bearing exotic fruit. And in front was the eastern pleasure ground: a lawn leading through single trees to a rockery and pond

The Road to Rockliffe

(James Backhouse and Company of York specialized in building rockeries), with a summerhouse prominently placed on a mound.

As the visitor walked around admiring Alfred's collection of plants, he came to the southern terrace. Waterhouse believed that ballustraded terraces such as Pilmore's provided a vital link between the construction of the house and the openness of the gardens. Standing on the terrace, perhaps with a game of croquet being played on the lawn beneath (croquet became fashionable in country homes in the late 1860s), the visitor had a choice of views at which to marvel. Again, and apparently deliberately, out to the west was displayed the railway viaduct (although Alfred seems soon to have tired of being overlooked by every passing train as a shield of tall trees was planted to skilfully obscure the mansion from the track).

Along the eastern fringe, a long screen of trees guided the visitor's eye over the ha-ha and down the parkland towards the river, with the tree-lined Yorkshire bank rising up in the distance as a full-stop. After many seconds drinking it all in, the visitor would have become aware that nestling among the trees at the bottom of the park was another construction: an ornate carriage bridge over one of England's mightiest rivers.

Our imaginary guest must surely have been so excited that he would have dashed back round the front to his carriage, before the coachman tidied it into the stables, and jumped aboard for a ride down the sweeping back drive to the bridge.

The first Pilmore Bridge was designed by a Darlington civil engineer, Robert

A 1950s postcard of Rockliffe by which time the majesty of the gardens had been lost, but you can still make out the ornamental gardens amid the trees

Above: The first Pilmore Bridge was carried on slender legs over the Tees in the early 1870s (Picture: DRO D/Wa 3/6/2). Right: A detail of the bridge's design from Skerne Ironworks' catalogue, published in 1879

Robinson, and built in the early 1870s by the Skerne Ironworks, founded on Albert Hill, in Darlington, in 1864. This Quaker foundry employed up to 1,000 men and gained a worldwide reputation, building railway bridges in Spain, Sweden, Ireland, Denmark and Australia. Its longest was the 3,852ft Kistna Viaduct, in Hyderabad, for the Great Indian Peninsular Railway in 1871, so the 204ft Pilmore Bridge a couple of years later was small fry. Still, it cost Alfred £1,730 (£150,000 today). It had a parapet of lovely lattice work topped by a rail of oak, and its wooden floor – three inches of Memel timber from Prussia "sheathed" in an inch-and-a-half of oak – was supported by three pairs of delicate iron trestle legs which had been hammered into the clay riverbed.

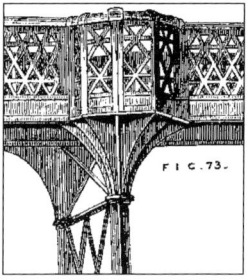

"The distance moved by each blow of the pile driver was taken as an indication of the dead weight each pile would be capable of sustaining," wrote Skerne managing director Edward Hutchinson in an 1879 book about all of his company's constructions. "The Tees at this point is of no great depth, but rises not unfrequently after heavy rain to nearly the floor level. The greatest danger, however, which threatens this bridge arises from ice, which, coming down the river in large floes at the breaking-up of a frost, is apt to accumulate at the pier, and exert enormous pressure thereon. The strength of this structure was satisfactorily proved soon after it was completed by the flood of November 1875, when the water rose 14 inches above the underside of the girders, and subsequently by a flood accompanied by large quantities of ice."

Pride inevitably comes before a fall. In 1879, months after his book was published, the Skerne Ironworks was declared bankrupt. Mr Hutchinson's health declined in parallel with his business fortunes. And in 1881, the Tees was again in great spate.

"At Croft," reported The Northern Echo on March 11, 1881, "fields have been transformed first into lakes, and then, as the water retreated again, into dismal swamps. The ground there looks as it must have looked when the Deluge first dried. The new footbridge at Pilmore, thrown over the Tees by Mr Alfred Backhouse to connect his two properties, has been carried away."

Undeterred, Alfred rebuilt. He used many of the same materials mounted this time on sturdier legs. In the autumn of 1883, he advertised in The Northern Echo for painters for the Pilmore Bridge. On September 21, their work was disturbed when they spotted a body churning down the swollen river. They downed paint pots and followed it for half-a-mile around the loop before they were able to haul it out. It turned out to be a John Wilkinson, a retired builder from Darlington, who had been missing from his home in the Eastbourne area of town for three weeks.

That drama aside, the completed bridge completed Alfred's vision. And from the steep, thickly-wooded Yorkshire bank – its darkness perforated in springtime by thousands of small, bright yellow daffodils planted by this leading member of the narcissus-fancying family – the visitor got a completely different view of Alfred's vision. The Durham approach was all about building up suspense by concealing the mansion and its out-buildings. The Yorkshire approach was all about opening it out and providing a wide panorama of an industrialist's mansion set amid a polished park where Nature was tamed – even one of her most raging rivers was successfully spanned – and her beauty was displayed to its best effect by the skilled hand of man. The ornate designs of Alfred's carpet bedding would show off his rare specimens, although the rarest of all plants in this highly-manicured paradise was a common weed.

This was a grand enough vision. But it didn't end there. There was another side to this botanical neatness. A terrible twin, wild and wooly, perhaps even a little overgrown. They were two halves of one whole.

The wild and wooly one was out in Weardale, near Wolsingham. Alfred's grandfather and father had both owned estates in the remotest parts of the dale, but those properties had not filtered down the family tree to him. So he had to buy his own. The vendor was his Eliza Barclay who was definitely his cousin but also probably his sister-in-law. Her father was Alfred's uncle, John; her husband was probably Alfred's wife's brother. Typically Quakerish.

Dryderdale as it is today, Alfred's wild retreat on the edge of Weardale

For all her wealth, though, Eliza's life was always touched by death. Her mother died on the day she was born in 1812. She lost her sister in 1829. She married in 1841 only for her husband, Robert Barclay, to die eight months later. Her sister-in-law died in 1848 followed by her brother in 1858, which left her to look after their son, a sickly 14-year-old orphan called John Henry Backhouse. She nursed him through London University and to the cusp of greatness, only for him to die of congested lungs in 1869 aged 25. Poor Eliza. The following year, she sold cousin Alfred the Shull estate in Weardale. Perhaps it held too many bad memories, for it was there that her father, John, had dropped down dead in 1847 at the age of 63.

For £15,000 (about £1.3m in today's prices), Alfred got Shull house, lodge and 477 acres. In 1872, he paid Waterhouse a further £14,000 to build Dryderdale, a Scottish baronial six-bedroomed mansion in grey stone with a steep slate roof and dramatic views down the dale. Dryderdale was a wonderful Waterhousian symphony of chimneys and an eclectic collection of windows, although the most eye-catching feature was the laird's rounded tower.

Waterhouse also designed the bridges over the becks and streams which wind through the garden, and a new lodge house, while Alfred laid out the parkland with sequoias and dug out a large pond.

It is a tucked-away country retreat, enveloped in trees on the edge of never-ending

The Road to Rockliffe

Alfred sojourning at Dryderale with relatives. Rachel, perhaps tellingly, is inside

moorland. It is remote today, yet it was probably closer in Alfred's horse-and-cart era: he could have caught a train at Croft Spa station for Wolsingham where his man would have been waiting with a carriage to take him the five miles over the Wear, up the steep side of the dale, over the tracks of the moors and into Dryderdale.

Yet it is internationally famous – or rather, infamous. During the 1960s it was owned by Vince Landa, the fruit machine king of Tyneside, whose employee, Angus Sibbet, was killed in the "One Armed Bandit Murder" of 1967. Landa's brother, Michael Luvaglio, was sentenced to life for the crime, and in 1971, the movie Get Carter was based on their notoriety and filmed at their locations, including Dryderdale. Michael Caine starred as Jack Carter, killing a prostitute near Alfred's pond, dragging her body across Alfred's lawn, before calling the police who raid Alfred's country retreat where an illicit card party is in full swing with birds, booze, and dosh scattered around Alfred's living room.

It wasn't like that in Alfred's day. In August 1887, The Northern Echo's North Country News section reported that Alfred and his Rachel were "sojourning at their beautifully wooded estate of Dryderdale". From one Waterhousian wonder to another; from one woodland beauty to a second: it was a tough life being a Backhouse.

10: The Illegal Member and the Pharoah's Daughter

WE can still marvel at Alfred Backhouse's eye for design. We can still touch his bricks and mortar. We can still sink deep into his opulence. We can still stroll among his woodland beauties. And we can stumble across the remains of his carriagebridge strewn, like Ozymandius' toppled statue, on the silty sand of the riverbank. But can we draw a picture of the man himself?

The few photographs show him stern and unsmiling, balding and bearded, serious and uncompromising. But can we get any closer?

In his professional life, he and his cousin Edmund, were in charge of the Darlington headquarters of the family bank for three decades in the middle of the 19th Century. They attempted nothing as daring as Alfred's grandfather when he bankrolled Edward Pease's fanciful notion of steam locomotion. Nor did they attempt anything as brave as Alfred's father when he opened a Sunderland branch after every other bank in that town had collapsed.

Their heyday coincided with the explosive birth of Middlesbrough – "the infant Hercules" as WE Gladstone called it in 1862. The new generation of Peases – Joseph and his son Sir Joseph Whitwell – were at the forefront, driving their railways into their ironstone mines to feed their blast furnaces, making (and losing) for themselves a second industrial fortune. Alfred's generation of Backhouses, though, preferred to sit on the sidelines of the Middlesbrough ironrush, concentrating instead on consolidating what they had, guiding it without drama through the turbulent boom and bust of the mid-Victorian economy and safely handing it on to the next generation. It was that next generation which, in 1896, took the big decision to amalgamate their bank with 18 other Quaker concerns to form Barclay's Bank.

Cousin Edmund also represented Darlington in the House of Commons from 1868 to 1880, and in 1876, he inherited his wife's father's fabulous sub-tropical garden at Trebah in Cornwall. He spent the next 30 years filling it with exotic plants and trees from all over the world (Rhododendron Edmundii is named after him). With these distant distractions demanding Edmund's time, it would seem that Alfred conducted the bulk of the day-to-day Backhouse business in the imperious £12,185 banking chamber that his friend Alfred Waterhouse built him on High Row.

In his family life, he met a bridesmaid, Rachel Barclay, at Edmund's wedding in 1848. They married three years later, but had no children.

The Backhouses, though, were a close lot, and Alfred and Rachel would have surrounded themselves with nieces and nephews – when the 1871 census was taken, five relatives from the Sunderland Mounsey family were staying at Pilmore.

The census also reveals that Alfred and Rachel could not have become lonely: in

The Road to Rockliffe

Alfred and Rachel inside Pilmore (Picture: DRO D/Wa 3/6/2)

1871, they had at least 15 full-time servants living on the estate and in the hall, and in 1881 there were more than 20, including a Biblewoman/missionary, Jane Hindshaw, 64, who lived in Pilmore Lodge with the gatekeeper's family. In 1877, Rachel advertised in The Times for a Lady's Maid, who had to be an "experienced thorough dressmaker, hairdresser and milliner" to earn her £28-a-year salary.

About half of the staff were employed tending Pilmore's grounds which Alfred liked to keep private. There are only two known occasions when he opened them up, both in 1874. In the August, 600 of the country's leading Quakers attended a four-day conference discussing Sunday schools at the Friends Meeting House in Darlington. Their Tuesday evening social event was a Garden Party at Pilmore. Being England in August, it poured with rain. In the December, Pilmore hosted a wedding breakfast for Sarah Aldam Backhouse after her marriage at the Skinnergate Meeting House. She was Alfred's second cousin, the daughter of William of St John's in Weardale who had followed the disconcerting Backhouse habit of suddenly dropping dead before reaching pensionable age.

Another who inherited the unhappy heart failing was Alfred's older brother, Thomas James. He died in 1857 when he was 47 and already a widower. This

WATER PARTY AT PILMORE
The oldest inhabitant had never seen it rain as it did on the morning of the Pilmore Garden party: it descended in a nice fertilizing torrent peculiarly adapted for turnips, but casting a terrible gloom over the minds of a thousand Friends, most of whom had come specially to Darlington for this occasion. Notwithstanding, however, the dilapidated state of the elements, nearly 72 venturesome Friends arrived about seven o'clock, and wandered around the moist but lovely grounds, attired in Umbrellas and Goloshes; others stood on the bridge making faces at their shadows in the water, the rest rowed about in a boat and sang "We'll Gather at the River".
Samuel Tuke Richardson

The Road to Rockliffe

orphaned his children, aged four, 12 and 15. The middle child was James Edward, who boarded at a Quaker school in Tottenham, London, and then went up to University College, London. On graduation, he entered the bank as an apprentice in Sunderland, and in 1869 he became a partner based in Darlington. He moved into Pilmore with his uncle and aunt, and so although Alfred and Rachel had no children of their own, they adopted somebody else's twenty-something son.

In 1873, James Edward married Elizabeth Barclay Fowler in Wanstead, Essex. It was a classic Quaker union as her mother was a Barclay, related to Alfred's wife, and her uncle was John Fowler, the inventor of the steamplough whose monument stands in Darlington's South Park. He had married a Pease.

The wedding gives us a rare glimpse into Alfred's nature. His wedding present for his acquired son was one only he could have devised: a £15,000 country house in Hurworth designed by Alfred Waterhouse.

Hurworth Grange is on the site of a gentleman's residence known as Hurworth Cottage which Alfred bought and demolished. The Grange grew on the site over two years, a typical Waterhouse house. Its eastern side was its main display elevation, featuring a large octagonal window rising to a square upper bay with chamfered corners – it is the same as an elevation at Girton College, Cambridge University, which the architect was building at the same time. The Grange's east elevation today overlooks a flat football pitch, but in James Edward's day, it would have overlooked the main formal gardens, which included a wooded Alpine garden of ponds, bridges and bogs which appear to have been constructed by cousin James' nursery in York.

To the northern side is the Grange's service wing with its enclosed court and back staircase. Its south elevation, facing the road, features a large, ribbed chimney stack, while the west elevation welcomed visitors with a substantial porch, a distinctive tower and a collage of gables.

"The decoration was achieved through inventive bricklaying with only minimal stonework giving an affect of solid well-mannered reticence," say Colin Cunningham and Prudence Waterhouse in their biography of the architect's practice.

This rare glimpse suggests Alfred, for all his professional carefulness, had a generous and imaginative streak within him.

Alfred's obituary writers in 1888 thought that his public life was as much of a closed book as his family and business lives. The Northern Echo said: "He abstained as a rule from taking part in public affairs and never sought those Parliamentary or municipal honours to which he might reasonably have aspired."

The Echo's Conservative rival, the North Star, said: "Though his name was very little before the public, Mr Alfred Backhouse effected a great amount of good in a quiet, unassuming way."

Neither paper was correct. In their rush to eulogise, they conveniently forgot the events of the 1860s when Alfred was "the illegal member", his name so public it featured in headlines as Regina versus Backhouse rumbled through the courts like a sub-plot in a Dickens novel.

The Illegal Member and the Pharoah's Daughter

Alfred Waterhouse's Contract No 381, 1873-75, Hurworth Grange
Large house of brick with stone dressings and patterned tile roof and stables.
Additional wing with billiard room 1886-87
Contractors: general, Parnell & Sons; heating and ventilation DO Boyd; stonecarving Farmer & Brindley; tiles, W Godwin, JM Allen, Craven Dunnill & Co (1886); stained glass, RB Edmundson, FT Odell; furniture/fittings, Henry Capel; iron work, Hart Son Peard & Co, R Jones; plaster ornaments, G Jackson; bell, J Warner & Sons.
Cost: £15,000; 1886-87 £1,500 (Picture: DRO D/Wa 3/6/2)

The Road to Rockliffe

Darlington's first real council was the Local Board of Health, established in September 1850 with 18 elected members. Along with three Peases, Alfred was one of those inaugural members. His elder brother, William, was the first chairman, a post he held until 1858 when Joseph, the head Pease, took over. The Board's role was to improve the health of the town: to provide clean water, to remove sewage, to regulate markets and slaughterhouses, to control building developments...

It actively fulfilled its role. For example, the Covered Market that in 1860 introduced Waterhouse to the town was the Board's bid to create a cleaner shopping environment where the fresh produce on the open air stalls was neither smoked by the polluting chimneys nor marinated by passing dogs.

Yet for the Board's opponents, the Covered Market and its iconic clocktower symbolised how the Quakers – principally the Peases and the Backhouses who dominated the Board – were towering over the town. During the 1860s, those opponents never missed an opportunity to bring the Quakers down a peg or two, whether by promoting theatres or by erecting war memorials – both concepts detested by the Quakers – or by thwarting their attempts to spread their values, such as temperance. The opposition coalesced into two groups: the Darlington Ratepayers' Association, formed by Nicholas Bragg in 1856, and the Darlington branch of the Licensed Victuallers' Association, formed in 1859 and led by John Wrightson, the landlord of the Sun Inn.

Alfred regularly attended Board meetings, although he wasn't the most vocal member. On one occasion, he spoke against the Peases' buff-coloured brick being used for the clocktower; on another he offered £50 to get the chimes in St Cuthbert's Church ringing again. More controversially, in 1866 he proposed "that in view of the appalling evils which result from the sale and consumption of intoxicating liquors...this meeting earnestly calls upon the Government at the earliest opportunity to bring forward a measure to remove the anomalies of the liquor traffic, and provide the community, on the principles of local government, with power to remove the evil when deemed necessary". Trying to ban the alcohol trade would not have made Alfred the toast of the Licensed Victuallers' Association.

Board members stood for re-election on a rotational basis every six years. Alfred was re-elected in 1852 and 1858. In 1864, he stood once more. He was one of 12 candidates for six vacancies. He topped the poll with 1,186 votes (there were fewer than 1,400 voters). Five out of the six retiring members were re-elected. The unlucky one was Mr Wrightson of the Sun Inn, who found himself 29 votes behind the 696 received by William Thompson, a fully signed up member of the "Pease Party" and, according to the Darlington Mercury, "an out-and-out teetotaller". In eighth place with 513 votes was Mr Bragg, founder of the Ratepayers' Association. So Alfred's side had triumphed over both of its principal opponents – a great result!

But Mr Bragg was not so easily beaten. He was a carpetweaver from Barnard Castle who became south Durham's Chartist leader. In May 1840, he was sentenced to three months' imprisonment for causing an obstruction and public nuisance in

The Illegal Member and the Pharoah's Daughter

Two men who didn't always see eye to eye: Joseph Pease (left) and Nicholas Bragg

Darlington Market Place. His seditious base was his grocer's shop on High Row (on the corner of Post House Wynd, a couple of doors down from Alfred's bank) where his opposition to all things Pease – like Alfred – grew to gargantuan proportions. When he spotted that the 1864 election appeared to fall foul of the smallprint of the 1848 Public Health Act, he commenced legal action, alleging that Alfred, the poll-topper, was not lawfully elected.

Alfred became known as "the illegal member" and the case, Regina v Backhouse, dragged on for more than two years. One hearing was before Mr Justice Lush in the Nisi Prius Court of the Queen's Bench in March 1866. Mr Bragg admitted that Alfred had topped the poll and if there were an immediate re-run, he would still top the poll. But, said Mr Bragg's barrister, the 1848 Act stipulated that the Returning Officer for any election must be the chairman of the Local Board of Health. He had to oversee the issuing of the notices, and the publication, distribution and collection of the voting papers. Then he had to ascertain which of the candidates had polled the highest number of valid votes. Should he be unable to discharge his duties for a reason such as illness, the Board of Health itself had to elect his replacement.

In the 1864 election, chairman Joseph Pease had duly overseen the issuing of the notices and the proper publication and distribution of the voting papers. But then he had suffered a deterioration in the debilitating eye condition which dogged, and darkened, the last decade of his life. Joseph had left Darlington for Ireland to consult a specialist oculist, leaving the Town Clerk, Hugh Dunn, to count and validate the votes.

Mr Dunn told the court: "After the voting papers had been collected, they were not

77

sent to Mr Pease, but a list of the persons who had received the highest number of votes was sent to Mr Pease in Ireland. The list was signed by the chairman and sent back to Darlington." Technically, Joseph had not personally overseen the counting of the votes, as was his duty.

Alfred's barrister dismissed this as a little procedural anomaly. He said: "The opposition seems to be merely having a dig into the ribs of Mr Pease on account of his being unfortunately afflicted."

Mr Bragg's barrister countered: "Nobody regretted the (eye) affliction more than he did but that had nothing whatever to do with the case… The question before them was felt to be one of vital importance, not only to Darlington but to every borough in the kingdom…because when an Act of Parliament appointed a person to be the Returning Officer at an election he was to vouch his character for everything being done in a proper manner…"

Mr Justice Lush came to the same conclusion as the other judges who heard the case. "His Lordship said he was of opinion that the election was invalid," reported the Mercury. "He thought the chairman had no power, if he could not attend to his duties, to appoint a deputy. (The chairman's) own judgement and his own mind should be required to ascertain the validity and numbers of the votes and, according to his own judgement and responsibility, who were the parties who had obtained the greatest number. In the present case, the chairman was not only absent, but he did not exercise his own mind and judgement."

It may have been a minor technical irregularity. Or it could be that the Peases, rather than risk letting control slip from their fingers, had been caught red-handed trying to ride roughshod over a law which had been framed to protect the delicate workings of democracy. The case went from court to court. Each time the election was declared illegal, Alfred appealed. The case appears never to have reached a conclusion because it ran out of relevance when the Board of Health was abolished. In 1867, another of Mr Bragg's anti-Pease campaigns bore fruit and Darlington was incorporated as a municipal borough. The Board was replaced by a town council with a mayor and a wider electorate which Mr Bragg hoped would sweep away the Pease Party. Indeed, his victory seemed complete when the old guard – Alfred "the illegal member" Backhouse and Joseph "the absent chairman" Pease – did not stand for the new democracy.

Twelve years after Mr Bragg's death in 1873, his role in local politics was proclaimed by William Wooler, possibly the most ardent Conservative Darlington has ever produced. Mr Wooler said of those heady days when Regina versus Backhouse occupied the nation's finest legal minds: "At one time this locality and district were wholly dominated by a self-seeking, insatiable, power-loving band. The only person who made any efforts to stem their grasping action was that Chartist, the late Mr Nicholas Bragg.

"Darlington owes to Mr Bragg primarily its municipality, for he worked single handed for years in preparing the way to overcome the overbearing opposition."

The Illegal Member and the Pharoah's Daughter

But for all the boasting, Mr Bragg was ultimately unsuccessful. Although the old guard did not contest the 1868 local elections, they merely handed the baton to a new generation of Peases, led by the town's first mayor Henry Fell Pease, and their Quaker sympathisers. Everything had changed, but everything remained the same.

Alfred must have considered himself emancipated. After 17 years sitting in a public forum to which he wasn't suited, he was freed from the tedious, time-consuming machinations of public politics and instead devoted himself to more private ways of improving the lot of his fellow man.

"He took a deep interest in everything that contributed to the alleviation of human suffering," said his obituary in The Northern Echo.

Alfred's prime interest was health. He was involved from the beginning in Darlington's first hospital, which opened in Russell Street in 1865, sitting on its management committee and donating annually, and substantially, to its funds – it was financed wholly by donations and subscriptions. Alfred must have been quite delighted when his first home in Darlington, Greenbank, was bought for £1,661 by his committee and demolished. On its site, GG Hoskins constructed a building large enough to act as Darlington's general hospital until 1933. Then it specialised as the town's maternity hospital until it was demolished in 1989.

Alfred was also an "originator" of the Fever Hospital which opened in Hundens Lane in 1874 to treat cases of typhus, typhoid, smallpox and scarlatina, the majority of them children, the majority of whom recovered.

He was also committed to the British and Foreign School Society's North of England College for Training Mistresses for Elementary Schools which first of all rented premises in Woodside Terrace in Grange Road but which expanded so rapidly that a £17,000 home on Vane Terrace had to be built (now Darlington Arts Centre). It was unusual for its day as it trained young girls to have a career, and was again funded wholly by charitable contributions, most of them, like Alfred's, of Quaker origin. "He was ever energetic in the welfare of that admirable institution," said the Echo obituary.

As a Justice of the Peace, he was noted for his conscientiousness, and in 1885-86 he filled the prestigious role of High Sheriff of County Durham. As a Liberal, he was commended for his "robust...staunch, thorough, unostentatious" views, although in the last two years of his life he split from Gladstone's Liberal Party which was advocating Irish Home Rule, and followed Lord Hartington into the new Liberal Unionist Party. Only a few weeks before his death, he attended a campaign meeting in Newcastle on the subject. So for all that he appeared to be a closed book, the creator of Pilmore had an open, lively and generous life.

He died, having just "fitted up" Pilmore with the electric light, at Dryderdale on September 2, 1888, in typical Backhouse fashion. Suddenly.

The North Star was prosaic: "At night, when he was preparing for the night's repose, he was suddenly stricken by the hand of Death and, after lingering only a few moments, entered into his eternal rest."

The Road to Rockliffe

The Northern Echo was more precise: "On Sunday morning, he attended the Friends Meeting House, Newgate Street, Bishop Auckland, where he was observed to be looking extremely well. Returning to Dryderdale, he took walking exercise during the day with his kinsman, Mr CJ Backhouse, St John's, Wolsingham. At night he read the family prayers and had retired to his dressing room, his butler having left him only for a few minutes, when a heavy fall was heard by Mrs Backhouse. On reaching her husband's room, she found him at full length on the floor, quite dead."

Heart disease, said the Echo, was the obvious cause.

On the Thursday, said the North Star, "the body, which was encased in a metallic shell, enclosed in a handsome polished oak coffin, with brass furniture...was removed by road from Dryderdale to Pilmore Hall, Croft" in preparation for the following day's funeral.

"The relatives of the deceased had desired that the funeral should be as simple as possible, and sought to limit the dimensions of the line of carriages by suggesting that those friends who wished to pay the last mark of respect to the deceased should assemble at the Friends Meeting House in Skinngergate," said the paper. "Nevertheless, when the sad procession, which left Pilmore Hall at two o'clock, reached Grange Road, Darlington, it was of considerable length, and about 20 carriages followed the hearse, evidence of the general respect in which the deceased was held.

"At Blackwell Grange, the servants alighted from the brakes in which they had ridden from Pilmore Hall, and the cortege being joined by about 25 members of the police force under the charge of Inspector Goodman, officials from the branches of the bank and others, proceeded to Skinnergate."

This "limited" procession was a long one fronted by 25 policemen and a larger number of bank officials. Then came the coffin itself followed by six crowded family carriages, widow Rachel plus James Edward and Elizabeth from Hurworth Grange being the principal mourners. Then came countless carriages of friends.

"The cortege was of very great length as it passed on towards the Meeting House being also added to as it approached," said the Darlington and Stockton Times. "Skinnergate was crowded with sympathetic spectators, and a hushed silence prevailed as the hearse was drawn up at the door and the oaken coffin borne into the Meeting House. For some minutes it was rested on a trestle, until the mourners had dismounted from the conveyances and taken up their place in the covered way leading to the graveside. The grave was situate in the centre of the burial place, next to the vault of Mr Jno. H Backhouse and Mrs Barclay. It was a great depth, and was prepared by Messrs McKenzie."

What a great depth of detail! The Jonathan was Alfred's uncle who had lived at Polam Hall, had headed the bank and who was father of Edmund, the MP. The Mrs Barclay was Eliza, Jonathan's daughter, from whom Alfred had bought Dryderdale and from whom he had inherited more land beside the Tees in Blackwell.

"At last," continued the D&ST, "when all had assembled the body was carried to the grave side, followed closely by the widow of the deceased gentleman, who was supported on the arm of Mr Edmund Backhouse and sustained by the presence of her sister, Mrs H Fowler. These two ladies were provided with seats near the grave. A long silence ensured. Then the coffin was lowered into the vault, and again the silence became almost as one that could be felt."

The Liberal-supporting Echo said there was "a widespread feeling of absolute dismay" at Alfred's demise, but far more instructive is The North Star's reaction. Only three years earlier, its proprietor had accused "the illegal member" of being part of "a self-seeking, insatiable, power-loving band". Now it concluded: "His loss will be greatly felt in Darlington and the neighbourhood with which he was so long associated and where his sterling worth was known and appreciated. The deceased gentleman was highly esteemed and respected by all who were acquainted with him."

In his will, he left £369,911 1s 1d – roughly £36 million in 2010, according to the Bank of England's Inflation Calculator. In comparison, Joseph Pease, whose statue stands in High Row, as he was the head of the other great Darlington Quaker family

Alfred's known spending: 1861-4, Pilmore phase one: £14,335; 1870, Shull: £15,000; 1872, Dryderdale construction: £14,000; purchase of 92 acres of Hurworth Farm: £16,000; 1873, Pilmore Bridge: £1,730; 1873-7, Pilmore phase two: £15,000; 1875, purchase of Hurworth Cottage and construction of Hurworth Grange: £15,000; 1875-6 extension at Grange, £1,500.

His other unknown major expenditure: *1860, purchase of Pilmore; 1881, purchase of the Spoilbank and land now occupied by Croft Spa Working Men's Club from the Chaytor family of Croft; 1883, rebuilding Pilmore Bridge.*

of industrialists, left a mere £320,000 in 1872 (£27 million in 2010). This also disproves any theory that Alfred had dropped the third, clocktower phase of Pilmore because he had run out of money. For a banker who was known to be sensible, he had spent extravagantly on the Hurworth estate – about £100,000 (just under £9 million in 2010) in only 15 years – but surely someone of his wealth in his trade could have raised another few thousand pounds if he had really wanted to finish it off.

His fortune was split between his two partners and nephews at the bank: James Edward inherited Pilmore, and Edward Backhouse Mounsey, another of Alfred's nephews via his late sister, Lucy, inherited the Blackwell estates. The granddaughters of EB Mounsey, Margaret Pratt and Dorothy Mounsey, opened the Rockliffe hotel complex in late 2009.

Of course, widow Rachel was allowed to live at Pilmore for the rest of her days. Indeed, she outlived her intended heir James Edward in the Grange.

According to The Northern Echo, James Edward "was a man widely known and respected, although of retiring disposition. Apart from banking and an interest as partner in the Etherley collieries, he was engaged in few of the commercial undertakings in and around Darlington, and never took any active part in public affairs".

Instead, James Edward seems to have devoted himself to the arts. He painted and exhibited at the Royal Watercolour Society. He etched, printed and designed jewellery; he studied the artist JMW Turner and the art critic John Ruskin.

Alfred and Rachel's headstone in the Friends Meeting House graveyard in Darlington

Like all Backhouses, James Edward was troubled by his health. To escape the harsh Hurworth winters, he took a villa in Borglihera on the north-west Italian coast, near Nice, where he visited the fantasy novelist George MacDonald who also stayed there. MacDonald was a mentor of Lewis Carroll, whose family home was at Croft-on-Tees until 1868, and a friend of Ruskin. Perhaps it was these connections that allowed James Edward a toehold in literary circles, because it is said that somehow, about 1890, Rudyard Kipling stayed with him at Hurworth Grange. The story goes that Kipling, in his mid-twenties and already acclaimed, walked with James Edward over to Pilmore where his eye alighted upon one of the great hall's greatest curios: a Roman sarcophagus.

James Edward no doubt told of the stone sarcophagus' folklore, of how it was supposedly unearthed in the late 1830s by navvies digging the mainline between Darlington and York. Stories abound about where it was found. Most likely is that it was one of two, or three, unearthed at Northallerton where, to the west of the town,

Castle Hills had long been rumoured to be the site of a Roman encampment. As the railway was driven through this huge manmade hump, Roman coins and pottery spilled out. The most notable find was a Votive Altar apparently made by the Sixth Legion which came to the area in 122AD.

Rudyard Kipling invented a folklore for the occupant of the stone sarcophagus, which he published as a poem entitled The Roman Centurion's Song in 1911. He imagined the occupant had been born amid the warmth of Rome, surrounded by culture and civilization. He saw him joining the army and being sent to the most northerly, frozen outpost of the empire, surrounded by pagans and heathens. Northumbria was a world away from Rome and after a lifetime away, in which he had acquired a wife, a son and a home from Rome, Kipling has the centurion being ordered "home". In the poem, the centurion pleads with his commander to be allowed to stay. It concludes:

Legate, I come to you in tears – My cohort ordered home!
I've served in Britain forty years. What should I do in Rome?
Here is my heart, my soul, my mind – the only life I know,
I cannot leave it all behind. Command me not to go!

The centurion's pleadings obviously worked and he was allowed to stay, and so die, in the cold Northumbria he had come to regard as home. Ironically, it was as James Edward was preparing in October 1897 to travel from the chill of Hurworth Grange to the warmth of Italy for the sake of his health that the old Backhouse family failing resurfaced. The Northern Echo reported: "Mr Backhouse had reason to go upstairs, and a few minutes later was observed to reel forward by the butler who instantly caught him in his arms, but Mr Backhouse a few minutes later expired from failure of the heart's action."

He was only 52. "The deceased gentleman had experienced indifferent health

The Roman sarcophagus at Rockliffe, which is said to have inspired Rudyard Kipling

The Road to Rockliffe

The partners in Backhouses Bank in 1896: Jonathan Edmund Backhouse; Edmund Backhouse, who was Alfred's partner; James Edward Backhouse of Hurworth Grange, who was Alfred's co-heir; and Edward Backhouse Mounsey, Alfred's other co-heir

during the past three years, and had watered in Italy for the past five years, and yesterday morning he was superintending the packing of his portmanteau by his butler, ready for departing next week, when he was seized with a sudden faintness and passed quietly away," said the D&ST.

He left his wife, Elizabeth, and their ten children, the youngest of whom was eight. Elizabeth lived on at the Grange until 1911, bringing up her family and working in the community. She had built a village hall (now the Christadelphian Hall) on the banktop above the mainline railway, and there she organized Bands of Hope, a Women's Adult School and a variety of social clubs. She was the founder and president of Hurworth branch of the British Women's Temperance Association, as well as being "a most munificent benefactor" of Darlington Hospital, "largely instrumental in securing one of the most important of operating theatres".

Because of Elizabeth's husband's premature death, it fell to her to act as executrix of Rachel's will when she died at Pilmore on January 15, 1898. Alfred's widow had endured many years of delicate health.

The Echo said: "She was of quiet retiring nature who took practically no part in public life being, however, of a kindly and benevolent disposition." She had recently donated an extra £1,000 to the hospital, on top of her annual contribution, to help provide a children's wing, and she also supported a girls' home in Kendrew Street, the Darlington Maternity Charity, the Darlington Sick Nursing Society and the

Darlington Christian Visiting Society. Rachel was one of the last of the three generations of Backhouses and Peases who had driven the Tees Valley through an era of enormous industrial change and revenue-generation: the Peases had performed dynamically in the front, although they were just four years from an almighty crash, while the Backhouses had kept the bank steady at the back. By the close of the 19th Century, their prominent figures had passed away and their great estates were being broken up and built upon.

Rachel's death provided the opportunity for one last grand but sorrowful funeral at the Friends Meeting House in Skinnergate. "The sad procession left Pilmore Hall . . . and was followed by a score of carriages," said the Echo.

"When all were gathered at the graveside, Mr JB Hodgkin offered a prayer," continued the North Star. "The coffin bore one solitary wreath: 'From the sorrowing household, Pilmore Hall.' The remains were enclosed in a patent metallic shell, the outer coffin being of fumigated oak, minus fittings apart from the plate. On this was the following inscription: 'Rachel Backhouse died on 15th of the 11th month of 1898 aged 72'. The grave was lined with ivy, evergreens, white chrysanthemums and moss."

Her personal estate – despite Alfred having disposed of all their property in his will – was £31,102 4s 11d (slightly over £3 million in 2010, according to the inflation calculator). She scattered it around her large family – Backhouses, Barclays, Mounseys were all beneficiaries. "Her consumable shares, horses and carriages, and outdoor effects are bequeathed to Elizabeth Barclay Backhouse of Hurworth Grange," said the local papers.

But Rachel didn't forget the ordinary people who had helped run her estates. "To her companion, Mary Elizabeth Currie, £1,000; to her Bible woman Jane Hindshaw, £30; to her butler, William Chapman, and to her gardener Robert Simpson, £200 each; to Ellen Gargett, her housekeeper at Dryderdale, £30; to Elizabeth McCombie and Isabella Steel, £50 each; to her maid servants of ten years service, £30 each; to her maid servants and footmen of two years service, £25 each; to her groom, John Scrivener, and gamekeeper, Thomas Fraser, £50 each, and to her woodman, George Cranston, £30."

But in death the Backhouses of Pilmore are revealed. Their closed book falls wide open. In March 1899, all their worldly possessions were spread out around Pilmore for the great unwashed to neb at and for wealthy to bid for.

The sale was held over four days, the Tuesday and Wednesday dedicated to furniture and household possessions: "VALUABLE ROSEWOOD CABINETS, 5ft to 6ft wide, with panels in silk work, and in plain and mirror backs . . . LARGE AND COSTLY CENTRE OTTOMAN in Silk Damask, with extra cushions; Handsome Girandole mirrors, in walnut framing; Mantel and Pier Glasses, Candelabra, in brass . . . HANDSOME LOUIS XV TABLE in Rosewood, of fine bold design and excellent workmanship; Excellent Mantel Clocks, Handsome Pillar Screen and Yable of Lac-japaned work, richly gilt . . . COSTLY BRUSSELS HALL CARPET of handsome patterning and special manufacture, 240 yards or thereabouts (this will probably sold in parts) . . . Spanish Mahogany Hall Table and Chairs, Footstools and Hassocks, Dinner Gong in oak frame . . . ANTIQUE HIGH-BACK CARVED CHAIRS of oak, in superior designs, seats stuffed and covered in crimson velvet; Antique brass-faced clock in old carving, Four-fold Oak Screen in plate glass; Antique Mahogany Chippendale Table . . . COSTLY ORNAMENTAL ARTICLES, large Oriental and Crackle Vases and Bowls, Linthorpe Ware, Majolica Ware, Plaques, Jardinet Pots, Hiroshima Bronzes, Benares Vase . . ."

The lots went on and on, and on the Thursday the bidders returned for the "VALUABLE CARRIAGES AND HARNESS, Excellent Brougham, by Hooper and Co, London; Landau and Clarence, both by Adelbertt, Long Acre, in good order with lamps, fittings &c, complete; 4-wheeled Dog Cart, in good order; Governess Car; costly Invalid Carriage, by J Ward, Leicester Square, of the best quality and style, with extra shafts for pony, recently new . . ."

In the afternoon, attention turned to Alfred and Rachel's oil paintings and watercolours which they had once chosen to adorn the walls of their palatial hall. There were mists, mountains and lakes, and plenty of lowing cattle. Two large views of Jungfrau and Monte Rosa, in the Swiss Alps, and Lake Iseo in Lombardy, Italy, hint at a fondly-remembered foreign holiday, while closer to home there were views of Folkestone Harbour, Derwentwater in Winter and "On the Tees" at Middleton-in-Teesdale. The artists were usually contemporary and they specialised in naturalistic landscapes. James Peel, for instance, had been their neighbour when he lived at Bransom House and they were down Woodland Road at Greenbank. He left Darlington in 1857 and received a degree of national recognition for his rural scenes. Other fairly well-known Victorian names were William Callow, Samuel Prout, Wilmot Pilsbury and TH Gibb.

The Pilmore conservatory, now the Orangery, in Alfred's day (DRO D/Wa 3/6/2)

Friday, the final day of the on site sale, peered deep into Alfred and Rachel's souls as their 2,000 volume library was sold. "Poetry and the Dramas, Histories, Topographies, valuable Archaeological and Antiquarian Works, in sets and series, choice and rare Classical Books, Scientific Works, choicely-illustrated Books, in costly bindings, all of which have been kept with care and are worthy the inspection and competition of Bibliophiles," enthused the sale advertisement.

The Bibliophiles were expected to compete hardest for the Elzevir Greek New Testament (1624) and Jerome's Tracts and Epistles (1468-70). Some might have been after the black letter ballad The Lamentable And True Tragedy of Master Arden of Feversham in Kent (1633), a Shakespeare-like play. Others might have hoped for the complete bound sets of Punch, Vanity Fair and the Illustrated London News.

A fifth day of sale was held the following Wednesday at Thomas Watson's Auction Hall in Northumberland Street, Darlington. It disposed of the greenhouse and bedding plants.

And so a lifetime of wealthy accumulation was broken up into a million little lots. Alfred and Rachel's collection of furniture and art, so carefully and individually chosen, was torn apart by the dealers. Their books, including the passages close to their hearts, were spread out among the Bibliophiles. Their handmade hall carpet, perhaps made to their own design, was cut up into scraps. Their dear collected memories of holidays and favourite haunts were bid into disconnected fragments of bric-a-brac.

Only one item remained. The finest of the collection. The sort of piece that would grace the entrance to a stately home like Pilmore Hall. It was a lifesize revolving statue, delicately carved in white marble by an Italian master, showing a sensuous young lady cradling a new-born infant in her arms *(shown left)*.

It was carved by Giovanni Battista Lombardi (1822-80) in his studio in Rome. Lombardi specialised in large figures of religious and allegorical young women in tender poses with flowing gowns rippling around their contours.

87

The Road to Rockliffe

The Illegal Member and the Pharoah's Daughter

They now sell in the world's top auction houses for £100,000 and more.

The Northern Echo said that Alfred's statue was "a magnificent example of Lombardi's work, and represents the finding of Moses. The statue itself, which is of beautiful white marble, represents Pharaoh's daughter with the infant Moses in her arms. The attitude of the figures is most natural, and every detail of the figures and the costume is chiselled withy extreme delicacy. On the pedestal are two bas-relief panels depicting Miriam watching Moses, who is floating on the water in the ark of bulrushes, and the discovery of the child by Pharoah's daughter. The statue and the column of the pedestal are so constructed as to be made to revolve by a slight touch, so that the whole can be seen by a spectator standing in front of the statue".

In the Biblical story, the Pharaoh orders that all newborn Hebrew boys should be killed. So that her baby could evade such a fate, Jochebed asked her daughter, Miriam, to hide the infant in the bulrushes where the Pharaoh's daughter discovered him. The Bible does not name the daughter, but Josephus, a 1st Century Jewish historian, said: "Pharaoh's daughter, Thermuthis, was walking along the river bank. Seeing a basket floating by, she called to her swimmers to retrieve it for her. When her servants came back with the basket, she was overjoyed to see the beautiful little infant inside…Thermuthis gave him the name Moses, which in Egyptian means 'saved from the water'."

In March 1899, as the vultures descended to pick the bones of Pilmore bare, Elizabeth Barclay Backhouse, of Hurworth Grange, presented the Pharaoh's Daughter to Darlington Hospital in memory of Alfred and Rachel Backhouse. Alfred had donated much money and time, once he'd been freed from being an illegal member of the Board of Health, to the hospital which was built on the site of his first home. Over the decades, the statue became attached to the children's wards which was very appropriate given Rachel's interest.

Since 1989, the Pharoah's Daughter has stood at the entrance to the children's department at Darlington Memorial Hospital, commemorating the couple who gave so much. Josephus' final sentence of his version of the Moses story adds great poignancy to the Pilmore story and Alfred and Rachel's involvement in the hospital movement. He said: "Having no children of her own, Thermuthis adopted Moses as her own son."

Left: the Pharoah's Daughter, by Lombardi, now in Darlington Memorial Hospital

11: The Captain, the Colonel and the Lord

IN the middle of the 17th Century, the court of the restored King Charles II was a promiscuous mix of scandal, seduction, jealousy and illegitimacy. Such a heady concoction led, 250 years later, to two of his great-great-great-great-great-grandsons being wealthy enough to become the post-Backhouse owners of the palatial Pilmore Hall. They changed the nature – and the name – of Alfred's estate. It was still a rich man's pleasureground, still owned by men who enjoyed being close to the countryside. But instead of Alfred's quiet, studious love of botany, the new generation of aristocratic owners loved the noise of the guns and the singing of the hounds. The Captain, the Colonel and the Lord, who occupied the hall for the first half of the 20th Century, were sportsmen: hunters, shooters and fishers.

They changed the estate's name. To Alfred, it was plain Pilmore; to them, from 1902, it was the imperious-sounding Rockliffe Park, derived rather grandly from the Raw Cliff on the eastern bend of the loop where the scrub couldn't get a root-hold.

Two of the three were direct descendants of the philandering Charles II's favourite mistress, Barbara Palmer. Every time he took up with a younger model, he gave her a title by way of compensation, and so she became the Countess of Castlemaine, the Baroness of Nonsuch, the Duchess of Cleveland and the Countess of Southampton – although Charles usually found his way back into her bed.

By his queen, Catherine of Braganza, the king had no children. By at least six mistresses, he had plenty. Barbara provided him with one a year between 1661 and 1665. He acknowledged them by giving them the surname FitzRoy – an ancient name for the son of the king.

The first of the king's descendants to own Rockliffe was Captain Francis William Forester. He bought the estate in January 1898 less than two months after the death of Rachel, Alfred's widow. The Captain was descended from Charles FitzRoy, Barbara's first illegitimate son whom she had given birth to while Charles II was on honeymoon with Queen Catherine.

Capt Forester's grandmother was Lady Louisa Vane, the sister of the 2nd, 3rd and 4th Dukes of Cleveland of Raby Castle, near Staindrop. This meant the 4th Duke of Cleveland was Capt Forester's great-uncle and when he died in 1891, he left the Captain his favourite estate of Battle Abbey near Hastings, plus a large chunk of the city of Bath and 2,711 acres of The Bolton Estate between St Ives and Penzance on the Cornish peninsula. The Captain was a truly landed member of the gentry.

The second of the king's descendants lived at Rockliffe for 37 years. He was Charles Henry Fitzroy, the 4th Baron of Southampton, who was descended from Barbara's second illegitimate son, Henry FitzRoy. Lord Southampton's aristocratic credentials were further enhanced by his marriage, in 1892, to Lady Hilda Dundas, the daughter of the 1st Marquess of Zetland of Aske Hall, nearby at Richmond.

The Captain, the Colonel and the Lord

In between the great-great-great-great-great-grandsons was Colonel Robert Clayton Swan, who owned Rockliffe from 1905 to 1918. He, too, was a man of vast independent means. A clue to the source of those means came in 1893 when Solberge Hall, a mansion south of Northallerton which he rented with his new wife, caught fire at 3am on Christmas morning. The servants had to be rescued by the fire brigade, but Colonel and Mrs Swan escaped because they were at the funeral of her grandfather, Sir George Elliot, near Sunderland. Sir George had started underground in a mine aged nine as a trapper-boy, opening the doors for the miners hauling tubs full of coal. He'd risen to become one of the largest coalowners in the British Empire – in Durham, Wales and Canada. He even owned the company that laid the first telegraph cable across the Atlantic Ocean. When he died on December 23, 1893, causing his grand-daughter to abandon her festive plans and so escape the flames, his self-made estate was valued at £575,785 12s 2d – that's £55.15m in today's money, according to the Bank of England's inflation calculator.

With such wealth running through every branch of their family trees, the Captain, the Colonel and the Lord could afford to indulge their sporting passions at Rockliffe. The first post-Backhouse resident, Capt Forester, enjoyed the shooting and fishing. Indeed, the latter pursuit nearly cost him everything as he was away at the river when, on September 15, 1902, the hall burst into flames.

This was the second fire at the hall as on the evening of November 5, 1879, the Darlington brigade had been summoned to the hall only to find "that the fire had been extinguished by the efforts of the servants without doing any material damage".

Capt Forester was not so fortunate. His wife was dressing for dinner when she heard a crackling noise in the library. "On proceeding there, she found the chimney on fire," reported The Northern Echo. She called out the hall's private brigade which turned a "manual" extinguisher on the flames while the good lady rushed from room to room tearing down the most valuable paintings.

"Capt Forester, who was fishing on the Tees some distance from the hall, first received intimation of the outbreak about ten minutes to seven, when he heard the alarm bell ringing," said the North Star. "He observed to Mr Simpson, the head gardener, who was with him, that it was a peculiar time for a bell to be ringing, and upon getting nearer to the hall was surprised to see a cloud of black smoke issuing from the building."

The Darlington Brigade, under Captain Uttley, arrived within 22 minutes of being summoned and found the south-facing drawing and dining rooms on either side of the library to be ablaze along with the five bedrooms above.

"The rest of the building was frequently in imminent danger, and if the fire had got to the chintz bedroom it would undoubtedly have subsequently involved the whole place," said the Echo.

In pre-television days, a good fire was regarded as the ultimate in real life family entertainment. The clanging of the brigade's bells, and the ringing of Rockliffe's dinner bell, alerted the neighbourhood to the drama. During 1879's false alarm, the

The Road to Rockliffe

Darlington Brigade had "started for the scene, accompanied by hundreds of inhabitants", and it was the same in 1903.

"Of course, a large crowd had collected, including many pedestrians and cyclists from Darlington, who persisted in getting as close to the burning mansion as they possibly could, but who were repulsed sometimes by an opportune hose pipe," said the Echo. Working deep into the night with five hoses, Captain Uttley's men eventually triumphed, leaving "the walls intact but roofless".

"The work of saving the furniture and other contents of the house was smartly carried out by Captain Forester, assisted by many willing helpers and the servants," said the Echo, but five policemen had to be despatched by train from Darlington to prevent the gawping hordes from making off with any souvenirs.

"Amongst the recovered property were several of the famous historic pictures of Battle Abbey, formerly the property of the late Duke of Cleveland. The family plate was stored in a cellar underneath the mansion and was safe. The mansion is insured, we understand, for £30,000." (About £2.8 million in 2010 according to the Bank of England's inflation calculator.)

Two years after the fire, Captain Forester sold Rockliffe and moved to Salisbury where he died in 1942 aged 82. Into the hall moved Colonel R Clayton Swan followed by Lord Southampton, both of whom were devoted fox-hunters.

Fox-hunting may be a country sport but it was born out of the age of industry. Man has chased animals with dogs since time immemorial, but originally it was for food rather than pleasure. It was only after Charles II's restoration in 1660 that the pursuit of pleasure – and foxes – for its own sake became popular. The oldest North Yorkshire hunts date from this time: Bilsdale (1670), Goathland (1670s), and Sinnington (1680), of which Col Swan was the Master of Fox Hounds (MFH) from 1891 to 1894.

The Industrial Revolution changed the nature of the sport. The enclosure acts of the late 18th Century caused fences and hedges to be erected in the countryside, making traditional deer-hunting difficult and requiring horseriders to acquire jumping skills. At the same time, new ideas about breeding lines enabled hounds with stamina and a keen sense of smell to be bred.

Then came the railways. Suddenly, the grouse moors and the pheasant shoots were only an effortless train journey from London. When the shooters arrived, they demanded a decent supply of targets and so all the neighbourhood's foxes had to be eradicated. The railways helped here, too, as they enabled huntsmen to move horses and hounds over long distances to join in the eradication. The popularity of the country grew due to the innovations of industry. It was the railways that drew the country sports lovers to Rockliffe, just as they had attracted Alfred Backhouse. Every year, the Colonel and the Lord paid the North Eastern Railway Company £6 10s "in respect of the approach to the siding and loading Dock at Croft Spa Station". Horses and hounds came and went at the loading dock which was slightly south of the station, only a short gallop from the Rockliffe stables.

The Captain, the Colonel and the Lord

Croft Spa Flower Show

To be held in the Grounds at Rockliffe Park
(By kind permission of R. Clayton-Swan, Esq.),

On Tuesday, August 4th, 1908.

Admission to Show :—
1 to 4 p.m., 1/-;   4 to 8 p.m., 6d.   Children Half-price.

A DANCE

Will be held in the MARQUEE from 8 p.m. till 2 a.m.
Admission 6d. Each.

The Members of the Sports Committee: Messrs. Abbott, Gent, Richardson, Roberts, and G. Stairmand, Secretary, will receive entries for the Sports up to Saturday, August 1st, 1908, at 7 p.m. Entry Free.

Sports to commence at 3 p.m.

Open to all in the Croft Postal District—Hurworth, Neasham, Halnaby, Stapleton, and Blackwell.

R. Clayton-Swan, Esq., gives 10/-, part of his donation as President, to the Children's Sports.

Colonel Robert Clayton Swan opened Rockliffe's ground to events such as the Croft Spa Flower Show. Below: the loading dock at Croft Station can be seen on the right under the bridge

CROFT SPA STATION.

The Road to Rockliffe

Col Swan, whose father-in-law was the MP for Richmond and the Master of Bedale Hunt, came to Rockliffe in 1905 in search of better hunting. "Unfortunately foxes were very scarce during his mastership (of the Sinnington), and this was the real reason why he resigned the position," wrote John Fairfax-Blakeborough, the doyen of hunting writers in this golden age of the sport when there were as many newspaper columns and magazines devoted to news and speculation about the hunt as there are today to football.

Rockliffe was surrounded by hunts. The Hurworth, the South Durham and the Bedale were close, as was the most prized of them all, the Zetland. A little further away were the North Durham and the Cleveland, which hunted at the foot of the hills with which it shares its name. The North York Moors were alive with hunts: as well as the three 17th Century ones there were the Derwent, near Pickering, the Middleton, near Malton, the Farndale, at Kirbymoorside, and the Glaisdale, in the centre.

Rockliffe was originally in the territory of the Hurworth. The Hurworth had started in the 18th Century although 1803 is seen as its founding date when the Wilkinson brothers of Neasham Abbey first kennelled a pack of hounds in their grounds. In 1861, racehorse breeder James Sawrey Cookson, of Neasham Hall, became MFH. His most famous horse was Formosa, which won the St Leger, the Newmarket and Epsom Oaks and the 2,000 and 1,000 guineas in 1868. But Cookson's most famous day was May 29, 1861, when his horses Dundee and Kettledrum featured in the Derby. Dundee started as 3-1 favourite; Kettledrum was a 500-1 outsider. But Dundee got badly barged by another horse and hobbled home second on three legs. Kettledrum "stole along from Tattenham Corner and came down the final hill into the straight like a flash, a sight not to be forgotten". Perhaps it was divine intervention: Pope Pius IX had a tenner riding on Kettledrum and the following day, £5,000 winnings was despatched to the Vatican.

Mr Cookson was replaced in 1888 by William Forbes, who had came over from Ireland without any connections. The most anxious moment of his mastership was in 1897 when there was an outbreak of anthrax in the kennels off Strait Lane. In 1911, after 23 years, Mr Forbes retired. This was the ideal opportunity for the owner of Rockliffe – the prime country estate in the Hurworth's district. Col Swan allowed his name to go forward as a possible replacement.

But the hunt committee preferred another candidate fresh from Ireland, Lord Southampton. On the one hand, it appears as if the Colonel took the decision badly, for he immediately quit Rockliffe for Lincolnshire and was never seen again. On the other hand, it appears as if he took the decision graciously because he allowed his victorious rival to rent Rockliffe from him for £519 13s 6d a year.

For "Charlie" Southampton, though, winning the mastership of the Hurworth might have felt like small consolation because he had moved to the area with the expectation of replacing his father-in-law as MFH of the Zetland. His whole life was dedicated to hunting. Born in 1867 and succeeding his father when he was only six,

Lord Southampton, of Rockliffe, with hounds outside Croft church

Lord Southampton was educated at Eton and Sandhurst. He joined the 10th Hussars in 1887, and headed for Ireland where he pursued more foxes than enemies as hunting was regarded as part of military training. He left the army in 1892, having just married Lady Hilda at St Patrick's Cathedral in Dublin – her father, Lord Zetland, was the Lord Lieutenant of Ireland in Lord Salisbury's Conservative government. Decommissioned, he put his equine skills to good use, being a member of the Freebooters polo team which won the Hurlingham Champion Cup in three successive years from 1894. Then in 1899, aged 32, he got his first mastership, of the Woodland Pytchley Hunt in Northamptonshire.

Being a MFH, it seems, is like being a football manager who learns his trade in the lower leagues while dreaming one day of taking charge of Manchester United. Lord Southampton moved up a rung on the career ladder in 1905 when he became MFH of Northamptonshire's Grafton Hunt, which had been founded by an ancestor and had been mastered by his father. In 1907, he moved again, broadening his experience as MFH of the East Kilkenny Hunt in south Ireland. In 1910, he saw his chance of managing in the Premier League: his father-in-law told him he was retiring after 35 years as MFH of the Zetland and suggested his name go forward as his replacement.

Lord Southampton, who was not well known in North Yorkshire hunting circles, moved to Blackwell Grange on the southern outskirts of Darlington to promote his

The Road to Rockliffe

In 1912, shortly after Lord Southampton had moved into Rockliffe, a biplane crashlanded in the front park. A large crowd pushed it into an appropriate position and it took off, using the slope down towards the river as a runway

case. Yet he soon learned that on the shortlist of well regarded local huntsmen was Lord Barnard of Raby Castle, the dominant landowner in the district.

He sensibly withdrew from the contest and found some consolation with the Hurworth. Renting Rockliffe, he built kennels within a dog's bark of his front door on the Rockliffe estate so that he could lie in bed and hear his hounds "singing".

In 1918, five months before the First World War came to an end, Col Swan put the estate on the market. The sales brochure acknowledged the conflict, saying that the purchaser shall immediately bear the risk of "damage by fire or hostile aircraft", but it makes much more of Rockliffe's sporting opportunities. "Hunting is obtainable five or six days weekly with the Hurworth, Marquis of Zetland's, the Bedale and South Durham foxhounds, also with the Darlington Harriers and a pack of otter hounds," it said.

The 659-acre estate did have other attributes. "A most desirable and compact Agricultural Domain with extensive woodlands and plantations . . . a handsome mansion house . . . delightful pleasure gardens . . . two-and-a-half acres of kitchen gardens: glasshouses, vineries, peachhouses and three gardeners' cottages."

But sport was the selling point. It was four miles from the nearest golf course at Dinsdale Spa and had its own tennis and croquet lawns, and as well as having so much hunting to hand, Rockliffe boasted "excellent modern stabling" which included "12 loose boxes, eight stalls, hospital and washing boxes, two harness rooms, three bed rooms, stud groom's cottage, kennels etc". Plus there was "exclusive salmon and trout fishing" and "really good shooting including Wild Duck".

Lord Southampton, of course, was the purchaser. An estate in the heart of hunting country had an owner who had hunting in his heart. Vanity Fair magazine, in its edition of March 6, 1907, painted a picture of the man who was known to the hunting world as "The Sinner": "Hunting is the absorbing passion of his life; he is a very strong and brilliant horseman, and if not the best man to hounds in England, there is certainly no better. He does not know the meaning of the word fear, and, unlike most fearless riders, he is without jealousy. To outsiders and acquaintances Lord Southampton seems silent, reserved, almost shy. At first people are apt to think that he is stupid and stuck-up. His intimates know he is clever, apt and amusing."

This picture is photocopied in subsequent profiles. The Lord is portrayed as a brilliant horseman lacking in social niceties. When he took over the Hurworth in 1911, J Fairfax-Blakeborough told readers of the D&ST: "If Lord Southampton has been impressed with the Yorkshire farmers, he has impressed them with the way he rides across country – a beautiful horseman, and nothing turns him! He is perhaps not quite as outwardly and boisterously genial and cordial as we Yorkshire folk like, and, as farmers say, 'hezzn't mich ti say fer hissen'. However, Lady Southampton 'does the sociable' in the field and everything is going on as happy as a marriage bell in the Hurworth country."

In 1922, the South Durham Hunt ran into financial difficulties. For a couple of years, Lord Southampton and his 18-year-old son, Charles, hunted both before fixing a solution. The Hurworth moved south of the Tees, under the mastership of Hubert Dorington of Kilvington Hall, near Thirsk, allowing Lord Southampton to

Lord Southampton and his daughter, the Honourable Sybil FitzRoy, at Hurworth Hunt Point-to-Point, at Sadberge, near Darlington

concentrate on the South Durham whose hounds moved into his kennels.

In describing the arrangement, the D&ST said: "Lord Southampton is a worker rather than a talker. He leaves Lady Southampton to welcome the farmers and chat with them at the meet. The master himself is a man of few words, and has a certain reserve which makes the reeling off of pleasantries difficult. Nevertheless, these same pleasantries often act as oil to the human machine."

Yet to the villagers of Hurworth Place, Lord Southampton was generous. For a start, he employed many of them – although because the 1918 sale had begun the process of breaking up the estate so he didn't own the houses in which they lived as Alfred Backhouse had once done. He created an allotment for them on his land, and a children's play area. Most noticeably, in 1919 he laid out a cricket square and built a pavilion out of estate timber so that his workers, and his son, could take on the villagers of Croft and Hurworth on home territory – since 1900, when the local fixtures were first played, the estate workers had always been the away team. In 1924, Rockliffe Park Cricket Club was formed and it soon merged with both villages' teams. His lordship was the first club president, although cricket never rivalled hunting in his heart.

His hunting career came to an unhappy end on October 10, 1925, when, during a meet at Fighting Cocks, in Middleton St George, "his mount got a foot in a rabbit hole, stumbled, and brought its rider heavily to the ground. The horse rolled onto the popular Master's leg and fractured it". This was his second break, and he was taken to Greenbank Hospital in Darlington for an operation, and thence to Biarritz to recuperate.

His comeback was to no avail and in 1929, he resigned as MFH. There was talk of his heir, Charles, following him in the saddle, but he was not comfortable with his father's privileged lifestyle. In his youth, it is said that he would climb down Rockliffe's drainpipes to escape the prison of his bedroom for illicit liaisons with actresses appearing at Darlington's Hippodrome (apparently, the driving reason for his father establishing the cricket club was to provide him with a different sort of temptation on his doorstep). Then, during the Second World War, young Charles was found sleeping rough amid the warmth of the Neasham brick kilns. In 1964, he disclaimed his title and went to live in Malta, where he died in 1989.

During the war, the army used Rockliffe's he grounds. They filled the stables and outbuildings with men and machinery, and from about 1943, a contingent of Canadian soldiers lived in wooden huts built above the Ring Field on the Hurworth side of the estate. After the war, these were occupied by Italian prisoners-of-war.

In 1948, Lord Southampton put Rockliffe up for sale. With Lady Hilda, he moved to Winkfield Lodge in Windsor where she died in 1957. He followed, aged 91, a year later.

Just as the Backhouse era of the wealthy Victorian industrialist had come to an end, so Rockliffe's time as a sporting estate owned by rich aristocratic descendants of royalty had now passed.

12: Pomegranates and Prayers

ROCKLIFFE emerged relatively unscathed from the Second World War, although its fields were peppered by crashlanding planes from nearby Croft aerodrome. The first to come down was a Whitley bomber on December 18, 1941. It took off, bound for Germany, but almost immediately, the liquid coolant spewed from its starboard engine. It couldn't return to the airfield because the runway was occupied by a queue of Whitleys waiting to get airborne. Instead, it circled until its engine seized up and caught fire, and it came down near Low Rockliffe Farm. Although it broke almost in two, its crew walked away unscathed.

Not so fortunate were the six Canadians and Irishmen aboard a Halifax which took off to attack launch sites of German flying-bombs on August 30, 1944. Within seconds, Pilot Officer Charles Clarke Todhunter – only 21, and from Ontario – lost control. He just cleared the Tees Viaduct before crashing into a ripening cornfield at the foot of what is now Middlesbrough FC's training complex. His plane ploughed a deep furrow towards today's Clubhouse. There were no survivors.

The third incident occured on March 4, 1945, when a Free French Halifax bomber was diverted from RAF Elvington, near York, to Croft. It was followed unnoticed by a Junkers nightfighter which opened up just before it landed, hitting it three times, causing pieces to fall off and flames to shoot out. The Halifax crashlanded at 100mph less than 200 yards from Rockliffe Hall, slightly to the east of the pleasureground. The crew managed to scramble clear, carrying out their unconscious pilot, Captain P Notelle, before the wreckage exploded.

So compared to this drama, the hall itself had a quiet war, and the fabric of the Waterhousian wonder survived largely intact. It emerged, though, into a new world of austerity. Gone were the days of multi-millionaire Victorian industrialists who could afford to lavish large fortunes on creating such stately homes. Gone were the days of multi-millionaire minor aristocrats who could afford to lavish large fortunes on up-keeping such homes in the name of country sports.

When Lord Southampton put Rockliffe up for auction at the Croft Spa Hotel on September 8, 1948, he was expecting a commercial purchaser. The sales prospectus described the property as "a comparatively modern and finely situated country residence seated in charming grounds and parklands . . . ideally suitable for a private hotel or for a school with its playing fields".

But the new world after the war also included the creation of the National Health Service. It came into operation on July 5, 1948.

On August 28 – ten days before the auctioneer at the Croft Spa could raise his hammer – Brother Benignus Callan and Brother Bernard Burke signed a contract on behalf of the Hospitaller Order of St John of God to purchase the hall, stables,

The Road to Rockliffe

Top: The east elevation of the St John of God Hospital at Rockliffe
Above: A Brother George collecting box, and Brother Richard and Brother Laetus, of the Order of St John of God, outside the south elevation in 1950

Pomegranates and Prayers

market gardens, Home Farm and about 200 acres. Their aim was to turn it into a hospital.

The Catholic Order had been founded in the 16th Century by John Ciudad, a Portuguese bookseller who had spent some time in a mental hospital. When he recovered, he resolved to treat sufferers better than he had been and he set up his own hospital in Granada in southern Spain. And so St John did God's work.

After his death in 1550, his followers spread across Europe establishing hospitals, assisted by popes, kings and queens. They came to England in 1880 when they acquired a 300-year-old mansion in the North Yorkshire village of Scorton – about ten miles south of Rockliffe. It became a hospital-home for more than 200 male patients who were regarded as incurables: "unwanted people" with mental and physical disorders.

With the start of the NHS, Scorton became a general hospital and the Order had to look for a new long stay home that could double as a tuberculosis sanatorium. The Brothers thought about Blackwell Grange on the southern edge of Darlington, but at £27,000 it was £2,000 more than Lord Southampton's home, where they created St Cuthbert's Hospital.

It was opened on August 15, 1950, by Arthur Blenkinsop, a Newcastle MP who was Parliamentary Secretary to the Health Secretary, Aneurin Bevan. Initially, the hospital consisted of the old hall – which the 1948 sales prospectus said had seven principal bedrooms, seven secondary bedrooms and four servants bedrooms – and the stableblock, which was converted into more bedrooms.

The prospectus also referred to Home Farm, a six-bedroom early Georgian

Patients playing cricket in the Rockliffe grounds while a Brother umpires

101

The Road to Rockliffe

Above: An aerial view of Rockliffe as a hospital showing the Brothers' chapel and octagonal recreation hall. Below: the stained glass windows inside the chapel

102

farmhouse, which the Brothers used for guest accommodation. They called it Pilmore House although it was the original Hurworth Grange. In the times before Colonel Gordon Skelly, it had been the most important building within the loop of the Tees, its past probably dating back to the 12th Century when it was the grain store for the Benedictine monks of Neasham Abbey.

In 1971, a corridor was built to connect Waterhouse's hall and the stableblock. The hall was renamed St Mary's and became an orthopaedic hospital, complete with operating theatre on its north side. The stables were known as St Charles', with the Brothers' living quarters on the upper floor and mentally and physically handicapped patients on the ground floor around the courtyard. In 1974, a third wing – St Bede's – was added to accommodate muscular dystrophy sufferers.

The 1971 corridor development also included a circular chapel and an octagonal recreation hall. The chapel, in particular, was a splendid building. It was blessed in November 1971 by the Right Reverend Hugh Lindsay, then the Auxiliary Bishop of Hexham and Newcastle, and it had a copper roof, a pine ceiling and walls of Teesdale stone. The wooden lectern, pews and stalls were made by Robert "Mouseman" Thompson of Kilburn, North Yorkshire, with little mice running all over them. A large tapestry, made by the Benedictine nuns of Turvey Abbey, Bedfordshire, hung from the gallery.

But grabbing the attention were the modern stained glass windows, made by Alfred Fisher, the chief designer of the 300-year-old Whitefriars Studio in London, who was possibly the most celebrated master glass painter of his generation. Installed above the altar to catch the southern light, they featured a sumptuous sunrise of colours.

They appear to be a collage of random shapes, but hidden among the hues are religious iconography and symbols – such as the pomegranate ("the apple of Granada") emblem of the Order. Even the transition of the colours has meaning: from the deep blues and purples of suffering through to the light, bright colours of healing and redemption.

Grabbing the Hurworth villagers' attention was the octagonal recreation hall. It included a bar which became a focal point of village life. The Brothers encouraged outside involvement in the hospital, through volunteer groups such as the WRVS, which ran a trolley service, even selling cigarettes and pipe tobacco from bed to bed. There was a Friends of St Cuthbert's group, which organised fundraising summer fairs and Christmas bazaars, and in the early 1980s, the recreation hall hosted a special event every month to fund the purchase of an adapted minibus. Among the attractions was the Spinning Wheels pop group – a reference to the musicians' wheelchairs – and a Question Time panel evening which featured the newly-elected, fresh-faced MP for Sedgefield, Tony Blair.

Further afield, Brother George Larkin became something of a local celebrity due to his tireless fund-raising activities. Every bar top and shop counter in south Durham seemed to have a collecting box fashioned in his own distinctive likeness: a

The Road to Rockliffe

bald head, a big nose, large dark glasses, a long brown robe and arms out-stretched inviting donations.

Times, though, were changing. Fewer men were committing their lives to the Order. From 1956, the Order had owned Hurworth Grange, Alfred Backhouse's wedding present to his favourite nephew, James. It had been run as a Juniorate, preparing 20 boys aged between 11 and 16 for a life as Brothers. It closed in 1968, becoming a community centre as it remains today, and over the road at the hospital, the number of Brothers fell from 14 plus eight novices in 1983 to only four in 1986.

By using more professional lay workers, the Order may well have been able to cope with its dwindling band of Brothers, but there was a bigger change within the NHS. The hospital era was nearing an end. Care in the community was coming in, with the emphasis on more individualised, less institutionalised treatment.

The Brothers had seen the change coming. In 1984, they had started their own Housing Association and had begun planning Rockliffe Court. It was to be an 18-bed supported unit when the less severely disabled patients could live independently in their own apartments. The Earl of Stockton cut the first sod on the northern edge of the estate in September 1987 and the first tenants moved in from the hospital in January 1989.

More severely disabled patients went to the long-stay sheltered accommodation in Lindisfarne Court in Darlington, while the most severely disabled patients who required hospital treatment were transferred to Scorton.

By 1991, Rockliffe was empty – of both the living and the dead. In the late 1970s, the Order's cemetery at Scorton, where it had buried its dead for nearly a century, was full, so five Brothers who died at Rockliffe were buried in the rose garden, within sight of the mansion's main north door. As the living Brothers retreated back to Scorton, permission was obtained from the Home Office for the late Brothers to be exhumed and they too were transferred to Scorton where demolition had enabled the cemetery to be reopened.

This wasn't quite the emptying of Rockliffe's own graveyard because, amid the pinetum only metres from where the Brothers had been lain to rest, Captain Francis Forester had planted the remains of his three favourite animals during his spell at the hall from 1898 to 1905. It seems likely that they were his favourite hunting hounds as opposed to his favourite hunter horses as excavating graves large for an equine would have severely damaged the tree roots.

At the feet of the tall pine trees, the small headstones had the animals' names engraved on them: Bluecoats, Castor and Pollux. Bluecoats, whom the headstone recorded died in 1911, may well have been a greyhound whose coat gleamed blue in the sunlight. Castor and Pollux were twins in Greek mythology who were immortalised in the Gemini constellation.

Capt Forester's animals haven't enjoyed the same immortality because by the time Rockliffe was reborn in the next phase of its life, their headstones had disappeared.

13: Erimus

ROCKLIFFE Hall, the five-star hotel with the longest golf course in Europe, a sumptuous spa, a celebrity chef and 63 luxurious bedrooms set amid a Victorian industrialist's mansion and pleasuregardens, was an accident. A fine accident, but an accident nonetheless. "I was having treatment for a shoulder problem and my surgeon told me about this place called Rockliffe Park," recalled Steve Gibson, the chairman of Middlesbrough Football Club. Mr Gibson, who had made his money transporting Teesside chemicals, had rescued the football club from bankruptcy in 1985 and, ten years later, was looking to establish it in the promised land of the Premier League. It had recently upgraded from the traditional Ayresome Park ground to the post-Taylor Report Riverside Stadium, and now the chairman was turning his attention to the training facilities.

Few other top league clubs sent their players to jail every day – practice sessions were held at Kirklevington Prison, near Yarm.

"We were close to signing for a brownfield site in Eston on the east side of Middlesbrough and I'd never been to Hurworth on the west," he said. "I drove over there and thought 'wow'."

This was early 1996. Alfred Backhouse's hall had been empty for five years. Its owner, the Order of St John of God, had received the Pope's blessing to turn it into a 100-bedroom hotel with a nine-hole golf course, but pennies don't come from heaven, certainly not in the vast quantities required to finance such a project. The Brothers approached Sir John Hall, the developer of the MetroCentre shopping complex at Gateshead, and Wynyard Hall hotel to the north of Middlesbrough, who also owned Newcastle United FC. He was unable to answer the Brothers' prayers and so the estate was on the market for £1.4 million.

Steve Gibson

Surveys by a quarrying company suggested there was enough gravel on the Tees flood plain for it to extract for 25 years, but the Brothers thought this was environmentally unsound and would provoke uproar in the village. So the agents were left to talk up supposed interest from healthcare and technology companies. In reality, though, a rambling, derelict hospital with a strangely extravagant chapel was proving a hard sale.

Until a man with a bad shoulder drove down the drive.

"So we bought it," continued Mr Gibson. The cost in October 1996 was reputedly £700,000. "We got planning permission for what we wanted to do and we developed the training ground." The Brothers' 200 acres – the footballers' prime interest – was

105

The Road to Rockliffe

Rockliffe Hall in 2010: Waterhouse's old hall married to the new

immediately turned into a state-of-the-art training complex, with seven outdoor pitches, an indoor gymnasium, medical and sports science centres plus steam rooms and a sauna. The local MP, who had been a newly-elected Opposition backbencher on his previous visit to the loop inside the Tees but was now Prime Minister Tony Blair, formally opened the £7 million complex on October 29, 1999.

"But the question was always: 'What do we do with the house?'," said Mr Gibson.

The Waterhousian wonder had accidentally come free with the land for the training ground. Warwick Brindle, chairman of Rockliffe Hall Ltd, said: "I remember driving with Steve up the long driveway towards the old hall and him saying: 'What do you think we should do with that there?'."

In September 2000, the club received planning permission to convert it into a 46-bedroom hotel with a golf course but it took another five years for the ideas to be honed. Market research identified a catchment area from the Scottish borders down to Leeds and across to Carlisle that would support an up-market hotel with attractions including fine-dining, a leisure spa and a golf course.

But Rockliffe wouldn't just be up-market; it would be five-star. Rockliffe wouldn't just be fine-dining, it would have a celebrity TV chef. Rockliffe wouldn't be an ordinary leisure spa, but would have a swimming pool bathed in the most delightful light percolating through the old chapel's stained glass. And Rockliffe wouldn't have a bog-standard golf course; it would have Europe's longest.

In late 2005, the club purchased the 400 acres of Low Rockliffe Farm so that, as it had been in Alfred Backhouse's day, all the land within the loop of the Tees was under a single ownership. This meant the course could spread a record 7,879 yards making it a challenge for even the furthest-hitting of modern golfers such as Tiger Woods. It would also, according to the club's promotional material, make it "the last word in sport".

It was all hugely ambitious. Total investment: £55 million. The football club seemed to have adopted the motto of Middlesbrough – "Erimus", Latin for "we shall be". Joseph Pease, Middlesbrough's founder, had used the phrase to capture the energy, aspiration and determination of the fledgling town that was springing up beside his railways, blast furnaces and ironstone mines. Pease, of course, was Alfred Backhouse's close colleague – it was his electoral oversight that had made Alfred the "illegal member". He first used "erimus" – "Yarm was, Stockton is, Middlesbrough shall be" – about five years before Alfred moved onto the Pilmore loop.

But there were many hurdles to overcome before the luxurious hotel could be. Firstly, there was the hall to restore. Many of its features – marble columns, stained glass windows, solid walnut doors, Waterhouse ceilings and fireplaces – had been boxed in by the hospitaller Brothers, and the roof remained watertight. But it had been derelict for 15 years, attracting vandals and thieves, while the plants in the Orangery had grown through the glazing.

To cover the cost of the restoration, the club was allowed to build 24 luxury homes on top of the tumbledown walled garden and estate cottage to the east of the hall.

107

The Road to Rockliffe

Waterhouse's beautiful staircase and the new pool featuring the stained glass windows

Then there was the new wing of the hotel to build. It was designed on the footprint of the old hospital by Darlington architects Browne Smith Baker (their company was founded in Newcastle in 1894 by Percy Browne who spent the First World War in America discovering the art of cinema-building with which he made his name in Britain) and constructed by Shepherd of York.

The romantic ruins of the old stable block immediately catch the eye, as does the sparklingly new two storey glass atrium which connects the modern wing with the old. Within the new wing is the health spa. It has one of the largest hydrotherapy pools in the country, eight heat-based therapy rooms, 13 treatment rooms plus the swimming pool gorgeously basking in the light from Alfred Fisher's stained glass windows that were rescued when the 1971 chapel was demolished.

Perhaps the most eye-catching of the new building's features is actually hidden from sight: the 100 metre long subterranean service tunnel running the length of the entire building and making use of the cellars where Colonel Gordon Skelly, the hero of Seringapatam, must have stored his wine more than 200 years earlier.

Then there was the golf course to sculpt. It was designed by Marc Westenborg from the Oxfordshire company Hawtree, and built by MJ Abbott of Wiltshire. Not only did it have to be the longest in Europe – average hole: 440 yards; the longest: the 7th at 640 yards – but it also had to be able to cope with a "hundred year flood" by the River Tees which is regularly reluctant to remain within its banks. Planning regulations stipulated that there could be no water run-off into the river, so three new lakes were built – the largest with a circumference of nearly one mile – along with eight manmade reed beds. Digging for the first reservoir unearthed Roman remains and archaeologists demanded that the course be redesigned to leave them intact.

Westenborg created wide, expansive fairways, with large, undulating greens and strategically-placed bunkers filled with English brown sand (as opposed to Spanish white). He made full use of the naturally damp surroundings by creating ten holes with water features. The green for the 5th is on an island in the middle of a lake.

"The trick is to make the course look difficult but play easy," he said. "Ninety nine point nine per cent of golfers can't play as well as Tiger Woods so we have to get this right for them. It's got to be a challenge, enjoyable and fair. We want someone to come here, have the worst round of their life but still have a thoroughly enjoyable time doing it."

But even with all the elements in place to allow the Rockliffe Hall hotel to come into place, unexpected events delayed it. The presence of pipistrelles in both the hall and surrounding trees stopped work for three months. As Rockliffe is Rockliffe where nearly everything is on a gargantuan scale, one of the biggest bat boxes in the country was built above the driving range to rehome the nocturnal fliers.

The 15 Roman archaeologists held up work on the golf course for two months and then seven weeks of some of the wettest summer weather resulted in the course being under water in June 2007 when it should have been under preparation.

109

The Road to Rockliffe

*Top: Dorothy Mounsey and Margaret Pratt, great-great-nieces of Alfred Backhouse,
open Rockliffe Hall on November 23, 2009
Bottom: Kenny Atkinson, the celebrity chef, in the Orangery*

Erimus

But no inundation, be it of a hydrological, archaeological or vesperian nature, could prevent Rockliffe Hall coming into existence. The first part to open was the clubhouse, its roof turfed so it disappeared into the landscape, followed by the golf course – although the dear old Tees again made its presence felt as only two days before the first players teed off in September 2008, the lower course was covered by floodwater.

The 61-bedroom hotel had its "soft opening" on November 23, 2009. The ribbon was ceremonially cut by Margaret Pratt and Dorothy Mounsey, the great-great-nieces of Alfred Backhouse whose grandfather, Edward Backhouse Mounsey, had inherited Alfred's Blackwell estates and had been taught the art of banking by him.

All that was left was the icing on top of the cake. That November, it was announced that Kenny Atkinson – the proud possessor of two Michelin stars, the winner of BBC television's Great British Menu show and the holder of the title Chef of the Year from "The Catteys" (the Caterer and Hotelkeeper magazine awards) – was moving from Seaham Hall to take charge of the main restaurant. Henceforth it would be known as Kenny Atkinson at the Orangery.

"I've had a number of really tempting offers from a host of amazing restaurants in London and across the world, but, quite simply, I was blown away when I first saw Rockliffe Hall," he said.

In March 2010, Graeme Storm completed Rockliffe's all-star line-up. The 32-year-old European Tour golfer, who was born in Hartlepool, came from Wynyard Hall to be club professional, he too enthusing over what he found. "This is the best complex, the best golfing facility in the north," he said.

Steve Gibson concluded: "It is an unbelievably special site." Which is exactly what had been said for more than 200 years by Colonel Gordon Skelly, Thomas Surtees Raine, Captain William Forester, Colonel R Clayton Swan, Lord Southampton and, of course, Alfred Backhouse about the land inside the River Tees' most beguiling loop.

Part II:
Along the Road to Rockliffe

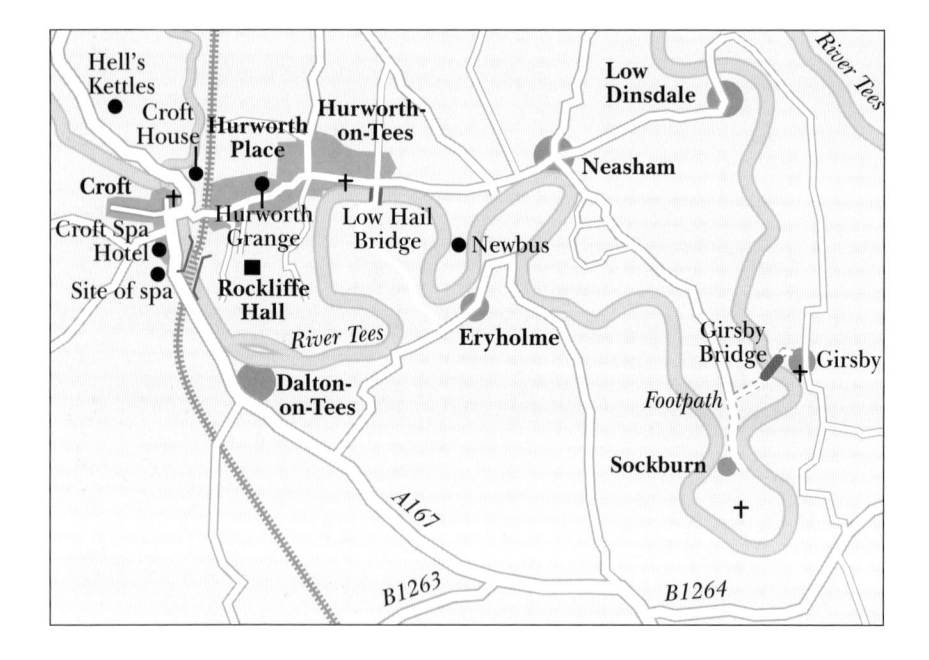

14: Croft Spa

Resound o'er Croft the song of praise;
Resplendent and immortal be
The strains to Health, which flow from thee.

UNTIL 1688, Croft-on-Tees was known as "The Stinking Pits" due to the sulphorous, eggy stench given off by the lukewarm water that came gurgling up from the centre of the earth. But then someone noticed that horses with swollen legs which walked in the stinky swamps and drank the whiffy water were miraculously cured. Humans tried the water, and soon it was discovered that it was particularly efficacious in treating ailments such as scrofula, diabetes and rickets as well as skin complaints. They quickly realised they were onto a profitable, fashionable venture, and by 1713, Croft water was being bottled and sold in London for "exorbitant prices".

The first spa tourist town in the world was Spa in Belgium which was famed for the health-giving properties of its warm springs from the 14th Century. Its Walloon language gave the town its name – espa, meaning fountain or spring. It gave the world an industry, and Alfred Backhouse's famous hall a future.

The people of Croft added the word Spa to their village name, and built a

An Edwardian postcard of the New Spa at Croft-on-Tees

The Road to Rockliffe

pumproom and bathhouse over the top of the spring. They found further springs – Sweet, Canny and Iron to go with the original, Old Well – and soon had a resort.

"When a healthy person is immersed in the cold bath he experiences a general sensation of cold accompanied with convulsive sobbings usually called shock," explained an early doctor.

"This is followed by a general warmth or glow upon the surface thus enabling the body to resist anything injurious. If the use of the cold bath be not succeeded by this glow upon which its efficacy bears but on the contrary be followed by shiverings, headaches, sickness etc it ought on no account be persisted in."

In 1808, the first Croft Spa Hotel was built beside the Great North Road, and 20 years later a hole was bored 26 fathoms deep in woodland to create the New Well. A fairytale path was built to it, criss-crossing the becks with dainty bridges and romanticised in the evenings by coloured candlelight.

"It is certainly an enchanting walk for any part of the day; the soft warbling of the birds, and the gentle murmuring of the brook, are enough to banish ennui and create

The Buildings of Architect Ignatius Bonomi (1787-1870)
He did substantial work at Lambton Castle, Durham Castle and Durham Cathedral, and built Durham Prison and courthouse (1810), Eggleston Hall, near Barnard Castle (1820), Skerne Railway Bridge on the Stockton and Darlington Railway (1824), St Augustine's Church, Darlington (1827), Dinsdale Spa Hotel, near Middleton St George (1829), Burn Hall, near Croxdale (1821-34), Windlestone Hall (1834), Croft Spa Hotel (1835) (above), Wynyard Hall (1845), Church of St Cuthbert with St Mary, Barton (1840), and Clervaux Castle, near Croft (1842-3, demolished 1951).

a forgetfulness of pain," wrote Miss D Wilkinson in her 1866 Guide to Croft Spa.

Those who were too infirm to make the walk could stay in the New Spa, a pretty building fronted by a trellised verandah festooned with roses.

"The New Spa consists of 12 rooms opening off a long corridor and including shower baths and a fine cold plunge, 5ft deep, which is supplied from the Canny Well spring in the wood behind," wrote Edith Harper in her 1907 booklet about Croft which she charmingly describes as "the Queen of the Yorkshire Villages".

"Bath rooms and dressing rooms are kept in admirable order, with every comfort and convenience in the way of carpets, chairs, dressing tables, mirrors etc.

"The hot baths consist of strong sulphur water, pumped from its source into a cistern, after which it is heated by steam. So strongly does the 'sulphuretted hydrogen gas' affect the atmosphere that it quickly tarnishes any gold or silver with which it may come into contact. It is this water which is considered to be the strongest in Great Britain. In colour it is a very peculiar dull, blue tint, almost like the colour of a jelly-fish, and of the same opaque appearance. If a glassful is exposed to the air for a short time it becomes almost milk-white, and forms a deposit of fine white sulphur. Its constant temperature is 52 degrees when cold.

"The sulphur water should be drunk shortly before meals, before breakfast by preference, one half-pint at a time being the quantity prescribed by doctors. This should be repeated two or three times a day, when in a short space of time the drinker ought to feel like 'a giant refreshed'. If drunk warm, a small spoonful of salt should be stirred into the sulphur water.

"Sit down on one of the benches in the pump room while you slowly sip the beverage, but first put a penny in the slot of the imposing-looking musical-box which stands at one end of the counter, that your soul may be soothed by the melodious strains of 'Whisper and I shall hear' or, if you prefer something more stirring, 'The Boys of the Old Brigade'."

So great was the demand to take the waters that in 1835 the Croft Spa Hotel was rebuilt by Ignatius Bonomi, one of the North-East's greatest architects, in a grand, Palladian style. An open-air swimming pool was built behind the hotel. The pool was filled in during the 1950s, but at the bottom of the nearby Monkend Terrace you can still see the low brick pumphouse that drew water out of the Tees to feed it.

The stroll along the London High Road from the New Spa to the hotel was part of the Croft experience. Miss D Wilkinson wrote: "Whoever takes their morning's walk along here in early spring when the air is fresh and balmy; the clear vault of heaven like a rich blue canopy overhead, and the glorious sun shining in all its wonted splendour, with undiminished lustre, and unimpaired power, as though it had never shone before; cannot fail to be struck with the natural gaiety and comfortable appearance of everything; on either side gardens and orchards are in full bloom, and the rooks keep up an incessant cawing whilst building their airy habitations. A shrill whistle from a railway engine and a few puffs of steam indicate the vicinity of the splendid oblique viaduct of the North Eastern Railway over the River Tees."

Taking the waters at the New Spa, Croft-on-Tees. This is believed to be Thomas Riseborough serving a glass of Croft's finest water fresh from the spring. The notice on the wall behind him is headed "Charges and Regulations of the Spas at Croft". It outlines the cost of bathing and drinking at the spa

Visitors were so moved by what they experienced that they penned poems of praise to the waters of Croft. The verse at the opening of this chapter was written in 1820, and this hymn was composed by the Reverend J Green a few years later:

If thou would'st from these waters all their virtues draw,
Thy health restored henceforth upon thy God bestow,
Then shall the purer well of Life thy solace be,
And Croft, sweet quiet spot, shall be God's croft to thee.

But there was more to the village and the hotel than just the water. On September 3, 1845, the Darlington Races were run on a new racecourse laid out on a field behind the hotel. The railway offered a special 6d return from Bank Top to Croft Spa, and Darlington was said to be deserted for the day.

Thomas Winteringham, landlord of the hotel, set up a stud in the stables at the hotel which at its peak had at least 22 racehorses owned by aristocrats from home and abroad. "In concluding my report of the Croft Stud," wrote an expert in the Sporting Life in 1865, "I have the pleasure to state that a more complete and better managed establishment could not possibly be, and every animal about the place is in perfect health and magnificent condition."

Croft Spa

The entrance to Croft with the hotel on the left and the church in the centre

Thomas had two particularly successful horses. The first was Alice Hawthorn, which won 52 races, including the Chester Cup, the Goodwood Cup and the Great Ebor Handicap. When it died in 1861 of "cancer of the udder", it became the first racehorse to be buried at the back of the hotel.

Then there was Underhand, born in 1854, which became the first horse to win the Pitmen's Derby at Newcastle three times. So famous was Underhand that it featured in a Geordie song about a jockey called Joey Jones, written by George Ridley, the man who wrote The Blaydon Races:

> *Noo when the horses started,*
> *An' was cumin past the stand,*
> *Sum shooted oot for Peggy Taft,*
> *And some for Underhand.*

Underhand was also buried behind the hotel along with at least two of Thomas' other favourites (Mowerina and Burlesque). The stables came to an end in 1886 when Thomas' son John, who had succeeded him, died at the age of 29.

Even without the lure of the horses, the waters still drew visitors – and the railways still carried visitors – to Croft Spa. The hotel and the bath-house took on new, pseudo-scientific names, and in 1897, the Croft Spa Hydropathic Establishment was advertising that it had room for 100 patients, and the Croft Spa Convalescent Home claimed to be fully booked with 60 inmates. Plus, there were numerous guest-houses and lodgings in the terraces on both sides of the river. But the fashion was already beginning to fade by the turn of the 20th Century. It was killed off after more than two centuries by the First World War when people stopped coming.

117

15: Croft Church

CROFT church lies low and lovely beside the Tees and at the heart of its riverside community. Indeed, one of its oldest antiquities is said by some to be a river god. He's tucked away in the stonework behind the main door, a curious carving of a man with a long arm wrapped around his head and another circling his tummy. He's a cheeky fellow, "rudely-carved" perhaps as long ago as the 1st Century. It would be so appropriate if he were a deity charged with protecting the community from the Tees' overwhelming bores, but it is more likely that he is a Romano-British fertility god.

There are also 9th Century Anglo-Saxon stones in the church – one, a cross shaft, with vivid birds and beasts bouncing around in the stonework – although the building itself dates from the 12th Century. A walk around the outside shows the centuries of construction, the crumbly red sandstone from the riverbed that the first builders used gradually growing into the sturdy and square ashlar stone blocks of the later masons.

The tower and the porch, which face south down the Great North Road, were built in the late 15th Century as a collaboration between the two most powerful landowners in the district to celebrate the settling of a violent dispute between them.

Richard Clervaux, of Croft Hall, was a coming man in Henry VI's time – in 1443, the king even gave him permission to send two ships a year to Iceland to trade whatever he wanted as long as he came back laden with "stokefysch" (fish). So grand did Richard become that he started calling himself "the Lord of Croft", and then in the 1470s, a series of violent quarrels broke out with his neighbour: Roland Place, of Halnaby, an estate on the western edge of the village.

The curious fellow of Croft

Cattle were straying on to one another's lands and being seized; Richard was poaching Roland's best servants; he was also hunting wily-nily across Halnaby's land and, worst of all, the two were at war over where they should sit in Croft church.

The dispute was settled by Richard, the Duke of Gloucester, sitting at Middleham Castle on April 12, 1478. He ordered that each man should fence their ground – "with dyke gwykfalle pale" – and drive their neighbour's cattle home should they

St Peter's Church, Croft, in 1866 when it had a square-topped tower

stray. He forbade Richard from enticing Roland's servants to come and work for him, and he ordered Richard not to "hunt, hawke, fische or foule" on Roland's territory without his permission.

And having banged their heads together, the Duke of Gloucester, who five years later seized the throne and became Richard III, declared that they should "holde thame contentent" for Roland to sit on the north side of the nave and for Richard to sit on the south side. As had been their families' custom for centuries past.

If either man broke the treaty of Middleham Castle, he would be fined 20 shillings.

To celebrate the outbreak of peace, Richard and Roland united to fund the building of the tower, sticking their stone shields on it – visible to this day – to mark it out as theirs.

The treaty profoundly affected the church's interior lay-out. The Clervaux Chapel of 1330 remained on the south side of the church, enclosed by a dark oak screen of 1430. When Richard died in 1490, he was laid to rest in "a tomb of the most marvellous hugeness, chastity and grace" in the chapel. His had been a remarkable life in turbulent times. He had remained trusted by kings over six reigns as the crown switched from Lancaster to York and back again during the Wars of the Roses. Even Richard III forgave him his little local silliness as in 1484 he gave him a tun of wine a year for life from his collection at Hull. In death, though, Richard is said to have revealed where he really stood: the epitaph and motifs on his giant tomb reveal his support for Henry VI and the Houses of Lancaster and Tudor rather than for Edward IV and Richard III of the House of York.

Less than a century after Richard's death, his descendent, John Clervaux, who was so "much giving to dicing, carding and riotous gaming" that he was called "the unthrift", had squandered much of Richard's fortune. He didn't even have the decency to produce a male heir, and so the Clervaux married into the Chaytor family of Newcastle merchant-adventurers. The Chaytors are still the district's principal landowners.

Opposite Clervaux Chapel is, of course, the Places' place in the north side of the nave. In 1649, the Place heiress married Sir Mark Milbank, Lord Mayor of Newcastle, and the family name changed. In the mid-17th Century, the Milbanks displayed their pre-eminence in Croft society by building the enormous two-storey pew which dominates the interior of the church with its dark, oppressive wood. The Victoria County History of 1914 says: "Anything more out of place in a parish church can hardly be imagined, but its merits as a piece of joinery are beyond dispute." It has a wide staircase up which the Milbanks would grandly sweep to their lordly box from which, through their luxurious red curtains, they would look down on the peasants (and the Chaytors) in the congregation below.

It was in this pew that Lord Byron is said to have worshipped in 1815 during his three-week honeymoon at Halnaby. His bride was Annabella Milbank. Although he fondly called her his "princess of parallelograms", he was driven into her arms by his dissolute, debt-ridden past which included a scandalously incestuous relationship with his half-sister, now pregnant, and a dalliance with homosexuality.

He hoped that "prim and pretty" Annabella would straighten him out – and that her £20,000 inheritance would do the same for his bank account. They married at Seaham Hall – another Milbank property – on January 2, 1815, and drove the 40 miles across the snow to Halnaby Hall for the honeymoon, or "treaclemoon" as Byron called it. Even on the journey there were tensions and bad omens, and the consummation of the marriage shortly after they arrived was hardly romantic. Byron wrote that he "had Lady Byron on the sofa before dinner" before falling into a

A postcard view of the interior of St Peter's Church, Croft, with the Milbank pew on the left

Croft Church

Halnaby Hall on the edge of Croft where Lord Byron, above, honeymooned in 1815

drunken sleep. He awoke with a jolt, staring through the darkness at the vivid orange embers of a seacoal fire. "Good God," he screamed. "I am surely in Hell."

His mood swung wildly while at Halnaby from bleak depression to tender affection, but still the people of Croft must have craned their necks to get a look at him when he swept up the staircase into the Milbank box in their church – his poem, Childe Harold's Pilgrimage had been published three years earlier to great acclaim and he was Top of the Pops. Byron left Annabella eight months pregnant in November 1815, and fled scandal and debt to Venice before dying in 1824 fighting for Greek independence at the Battle of Missolonghi.

He is not the only exotic visitor to Croft church, though. George Hudson, "the Railway King" was said to be a regular visitor in the 1840s when he was connecting all the small, private railway companies to create a mainline from Newcastle to London, before he was exposed as a terrible fraudster and collapsed into bankruptcy. If the sermon bored the Railway King, he would turn his back on the pastor while his wife would let her tedium known by putting up her parasol. It is true that sermons in olden days had a horrible habit of dragging on and on. Indeed, there is an hourglass on the wall by the pulpit to inform the vicar when time was running out.

But the rector that Hudson was snubbing was none other than Charles Dodgson, who arrived in the village in 1843 with his eldest son, also Charles. To 11-year-old Charles, the church was beguiling, entrancing and even inspiring: from the curious man behind the door to the birds and beasts weaved into the Anglo-Saxon carving, from the animals fighting and playing in the 14th Century sedilia stonework by the altar to the pelican and dragon carved in the early 15th Century wooden ceiling of the chancel, and to the peculiar faces on the gargoyles all around. Indeed, the boy reckoned that one feline-looking gargoyle wasn't there when you sat in a pew but when you stood to sing it suddenly emerged with a great big grin on its face. A Cheshire cat, he thought, as he collected bizarre fancies to one day weave into the most famous of children's stories…

16: Lewis Carroll

Fair stands the ancient Rectory,
The Rectory of Croft,
The sun shines bright upon it,
The breezes whisper soft.
From all the house and garden
Its inhabitants come forth,
And muster in the road without,
And pace in twos and threes about,
The children of the North.

AFTER Shakespeare, the most frequently quoted writer in the English language is Lewis Carroll, a rector's son who grew up on the road to Rockliffe. Indeed, much of Carroll's fantasy was inspired by the veritable wonderland of extraordinary stories he found on the road, stories of fire-breathing dragons, smoke-snorting engines, life-giving water, over-sized oxen, back-to-front writing and time-telling sundials.

From this raw material, he created books that changed childhood.

Charles Lutwidge Dodgson was a shy, stammering boy of 11 when, in 1843, his father was appointed by the Prime Minister, Sir Robert Peel, to be the rector of Croft. The family moved from a small, rural parish in Cheshire (salary: £191pa) to this large North Yorkshire metropolis (salary: £1,100pa) slap bang on the Great North Road, and right beside the world's first mainline railway which brought fashionable tourists flocking to take the sulphureous spa waters.

Indeed, Charles had only been there two years when the Darlington races were run on the village's new racecourse and Darlington was said to be deserted for the day.

Charles and his seven sisters and three brothers lived opposite his father's St Peter's Church in the Rectory, which had a garden large enough for an imagination to run riot. Out of a wheelbarrow, a barrel and a small truck, Charles made a train which ran around the gardens, running over his brothers and sisters before stopping as per the timetable at three stations.

There was a spreading ancient yew tree, a dense "tulgey wood" of shrubbery, and a night-blooming cereus – an ugly, stick-thin cactus from the Sonoran Desert, in North America, which bloomed for one night only (usually around May 31). Crowds came from miles around to stare at its weirdness.

The boy's bedroom was on the second floor where workmen had scratched their names on the outside of a windowpane. "Edward Johnson Plumber Darlington 1834", said one line. Of course, Charles inside needed a looking-glass to read it.

The Dodgsons were a huge, happy family, orchestrated by Charles – the third

Croft Rectory, which was the boyhood home of Charles Dodgson, aka Lewis Carroll

eldest – who created puzzles and games to entertain his sisters. He built little theatres to perform his puppet plays, and he compiled a family magazine to keep the youngsters laughing. The first was put together in 1845 and was called Useful and Instructive Poetry. It included a couple of limericks which, for a 13-year-old, showed great promise:

> His sister named Lucy o'Finner
> Grew constantly thinner and thinner,
> The reason was plain,
> She slept out in the rain,
> And was never allowed any dinner.

> There was once a young man of Oporta
> Who daily got shorter and shorter,
> The reason, he said
> Was the hod on his head
> Which was filled with the heaviest mortar.

For the first 18 months at Croft, Carroll was taught at home by his father – a double first in classics and maths from Oxford University. Then in August 1844, he went to board at Richmond Grammar School, ten miles away. The school was in St Mary's churchyard, where a car park is today opposite Richmond Lower School. For 100 guineas-a-year Charles got to stay with the headteacher, James Tate, in Swale House – currently occupied by Richmondshire council.

Charles spent a happy 16 months at Richmond followed by an unhappy four years at Rugby school where he continued to excel at maths but found that the

The Road to Rockliffe

rumbustuous boys and the fagging system did not suit his delicate nature.

In 1850, he returned to his family at Croft for a year to prepare to study maths at Christ Church, Oxford.

His magazine that year was called The Rectory Umbrella (named after the spreading yew tree beneath which it was composed) and contained the poem Lays of Sorrow. The poem mentions Ulfrid Longbow, who was Carroll's younger brother, Wilfrid Longley Dodgson, and it expresses his fondness for his home. It gives a clue as to the happy but studious life lived within the Rectory walls:

> *And often in the evenings*
> *When the fire is blazing bright*
> *When books bestrew the table*
> *And moths obscure the light*
> *When crying children go to bed*
> *A struggling, kicking load*
> *We'll talk of Ulfrid Longbow's deed*
> *How, in his brother's utmost need,*
> *Back to his aid he flew with speed*
> *And how he faced the fiery steed*
> *And kept the new Croft road.*

Charles started at Christ Church on January 24, 1851, three days shy of his 19th birthday. Two days later, he was called home. His beloved mother Frances had died, aged 47, of "inflammation of the brain". Some commentators feel Charles never recovered from this profound shock and so his emotional development remained rooted in childhood.

Rev Charles Dogson, photographed by his son Lewis Carroll

Gradually, though, his life fell into a new routine. Termtimes in Oxford and vacations at Croft, although his father's new role as Canon of Ripon Cathedral meant that the family decamped there for the first three months of each year. In 1854, Charles spent the summer at Whitby, studying maths and gaining a reputation among children as a seaside storyteller. The Easter 1855 brought him back to Croft, even walking along Darlington's High Row to Robert Swales' shop to get a book about Euclid, the Greek "father of geometry", with which to enthuse his sister Louisa. That summer, he helped his father at Croft school as a prelude to his own teaching and lecturing career now he had graduated. He produced another family magazine, entitled Mischmasch. It included, under the heading A Stanza of Anglo-Saxon Poetry, the first appearance of the most famous nonsense poem in the English language:

Lewis Carroll

'Twas bryllyg, and the slythy toves
Did gyre and gymble in the wabe:
All mimsy were the borogoves:
And the mome raths outgrabe.

In the "learned notes" which Charles attached to his "obscure but deeply-affecting poem", he gave a translation: "It was evening, and the smooth, active badgers were scratching and boring holes in the hillside; all unhappy were the parrots; and the grave turtles squeaked out."

He also defined each of his made-up words. A borogrove, he said, was "an extinct kind of parrot. They had no wings, beaks turned up, and made their nests under sundials: lived on veal". He added: "There were probably sundials on the top of the hill, and the borogroves were afraid that their nests would be undermined."

The verse was properly published in 1872 in Through the Looking Glass when it had become part of the Jaberwocky poem. The Jaberwock was an enormous dragon that required slaying with a special "vorpal" sword, an idea inspired by the Sockburn Worm that terrorized people who lived along the Rockliffe road until it was disposed of by brave Sir John Conyers (see Chapter 27). Charles would probably have seen his tomb, and witnessed the peculiar ceremony on Croft bridge when a new Bishop of Durham is presented with the Conyers' falchion – a special sword – when first sets foot in his diocese.

The sundials under which the timorous borogroves resided must also have been inspired locally by the 30 or so timepieces that adorned the south-facing main road through Hurworth (see Chapter 22).

Two months after the borogroves' first appearance in Mischmasch, Uncle Skeffington Lutwidge arrived at Croft Rectory. "Skeffy" was a great favourite as he was gadget-mad and, on September 8, 1855, he arrived bearing his new camera paraphernalia. He and Charles sallied forth, carrying all the equipment, and took photographs of the church and the bridge. On developing, the images were unsuccessful, but Charles was smitten. He became a photographic pioneer, and on December 31, 1856, the 80 children at Croft school enjoyed a two-and-a-half hour Magic Lantern show in which Charles performed 13 self-written songs illustrated by his new-fangled slides. You can still see the original Croft school, founded and funded by Charles' father in 1845, as it is now a private house, complete with school bell, next to the modern primary school in the village.

But the camera not only captured the subjects it was pointed at. It also revealed something of the soul of the man taking the pictures. By 1858, Charles was taking pictures of Alfred, Lord Tennyson, the great poet, and of Alice Liddell, an Oxford dean's six-year-old daughter. His portraits show great and ground-breaking artistic merit, but the preponderance of studies of young, barely-clothed girls like Alice is far too paedophilic for modern tastes. This photographic evidence, coupled with his close friendships with female children, has sullied his reputation, although there is

The Road to Rockliffe

no physical evidence to convict him of anything.

And although we may grimace at his relationships, he was undoubtedly adored by his child friends. During the winter of 1857, he visited his father's friend Charles Thomas Longley who had just been installed as Bishop of Durham. Longley's daughters entreated their guest to write a poem about the reputedly haunted cellar at Auckland Castle which they called "Scotland" because it was so cold and remote:

> *Yn the Auckland Castell cellar,*
> *Long, long ago*
> *I was shut – a brisk young feller -*
> *Woe, woe, ah woe!*

In Oxford, Alice Liddell and her elder sisters, Lorina and Edith, also enjoyed Charles' storytelling. Indeed, on July 4, 1862 – "a golden afternoon" – they went rowing on the Thames and Charles extemporised a silly story about the day Alice fell down a rabbit hole. Alice liked the story so much that she begged Charles to write it down, a task that took him a two-and-a-half years, editing out private jokes and adding and embellishing the scenes by drawing on his back catalogue of surrealities.

The handwritten manuscript of Alice's Adventures Under Ground gained such rave reviews among Oxford children that Charles published it properly in 1865 as Alice in Wonderland. The author was said to be "Lewis Carroll", a pen-name he had been using for nearly a decade for his fantasy poems and his academic articles on maths and logic. (There is a logic to "Lewis Carroll": it his middle name Lutwidge translated from German into English, and his first name Charles Latinised.)

It was so successful that within a couple of years he was planning a follow-up. Indeed, in June 1868, he was just completing a deal with Sir John Tenniel to illustrate the second volume when he received a telegram from Croft saying that his father was unwell.

He immediately set off from Oxford, but arrived too late at Croft Rectory, where his sisters had laid his father's body on a bed strewn with flowers and beside a cross made from roses. Charles said the death was "the greatest blow that has ever fallen on my life", and he took years to recover. Some say that Alice Through the Looking Glass – the second volume which he eventually published in 1871 – is darker than the first because of his subsequent depression.

On June 21, Charles buried his father beneath a heavy slab on the north side of Croft Church with the River Tees running perilously close. Tall metal railings keep young children from crawling on the stone, but they can't keep out the brambles which every year make their way across.

Suddenly Charles, this donnish mathematical lecturer, found himself head of a family of seven sisters and three brothers. And the Church wanted to install a new rector in The Rectory.

He immediately set about house-hunting and quickly discovered The Chestnuts in

Croft Church, now with a castellated tower, in 1937

Guildford, conveniently close to Oxford, where he settled his sisters. He returned to Croft for a last time on August 22. He held a sale of unwanted possessions, packed the wanted ones up, and left on September 1. He wrote in his diary: "Dispersion of family from the old home we have known for five-and-twenty years."

And that was that. He seems never physically to have returned, but mentally his memories regularly dragged this child of the north back to his happy childhood spent on the road to Rockliffe.

A plaque in Croft church dedicated to him contains his own wistful words:

> *I'd give all wealth that years have piled*
> *The slow result of life's decay,*
> *To be once more a little child*
> *For one bright summer day.*

17: Croft Bridge

STANDING on Croft Bridge, with the Tees rushing noisily beneath, you can feel the sweep of the years rushing by as well. For at least seven centuries, this bridge has carried the Great North Road from Yorkshire into Durham, with it all the vital communications between the great capitals of London and Edinburgh galloping across it.

On December 17, 1569, an army nearly 20,000 strong marched over it in support of Queen Elizabeth I. When the rebels leading the Rising of the North saw such numbers, they realised the game was up and faded into the Durham Dales.

Nearly 200 years later, the Duke of Cumberland marched his army – nearly as strong as Elizabeth's – over the bridge on his way to defeat the Scots at the Battle of Culloden.

Since 1790, the new Bishop of Durham has been welcomed into his diocese by being presented in the centre of the bridge with a falchion – a large sword – and the words: "My Lord, this is the falchion that slew the Worm Dragon, which spared neither man, woman, nor child." The new bishop, of course, will know the story of the dragon from just down the Rockliffe road in Sockburn which was slain by brave Sir John Conyers. The bishop, of course, will also know what he has to do with the falchion: immediately hand it back and courteously wish its bearer health and longevity.

In July 1819, banker Jonathan Backhouse snapped an axle on the bridge when he had £32,000 of gold bullion in his carriage as he made a mad dash from London to save his bank and the Stockton and Darlington Railway (see Chapter 5).

So many stories are etched into the local red sandstone of Croft Bridge which, since 2007, has been a Grade I listed building. The southern half of the bridge dates from distant medieval times. There may even be the foundations of a more ancient construction beside it.

The first real mention of the bridge is in 1356 when it was "in a dangerous state by the great flooding of the river". It was repaired. In the 15th Century – possibly in 1400 by Bishop Walter Skirlaw of Durham, who was a great bridge-builder – it was rebuilt and became one of the most important in the country.

In 1531, "the grete Bridge at Crofte" was described as "beinge of sixe myghtye large pillars, and of seven arches of stone worke" and that it was "the most directe and sure way and passage for the Kinge or Sovraigne Lordes armye and ordynance to resort and passe over into the Northe parties and marches of this his realme, over the surtie and defence of the same agaynst the invasion of the Scotts and other his enemyes".

Yet that year, a terrible flood had undermined three of the six mighty large pillars and "a great quantite" of the arches had fallen down, leaving the "good devowte

Croft Bridge

Croft Bridge, Darlington.

An Edwardian postcard taken from the Durham side of Croft Bridge

people" of Croft to pay for its repair. Between 1562 and 1580, they spent £184 on it but by 1616 it was again in a "ruinous and decayed condition". Croft Bridge was like the Forth Bridge in that it required a never-ending job to keep it standing in the face of the great Tees Bore.

By 1631, it was a still "great ruin", and so in 1651 local people spent £60 on it. In 1657, they spent another £150 on repairs. And again the following year they had to spend £66 13s 4d on its upkeep.

Croft residents felt very hard-pressed in having a tax levied upon just them to fund repairs to a nationally important crossing, so in 1673, the North Riding of Yorkshire agreed to repair 95 yards and two inches of the bridge while Durham footed the bill for the remaining 53 yards and two inches (today, North Yorkshire looks after the whole lot). This agreement is marked by a blue fossil-filled stone, possibly of Frosterley marble, at the boundary. It says: "DUN CONTRIBVAT NORTH RID. COM. EBOR. ET COM. DUNEL. STATV. APVD SESS. VTRQE GEN. PAC. AN. DO. 1673" ("Let Durham with the North Riding contribute in the upkeep among themselves in proportion.")

It would say that if you could read it. The blue stone was on the pavement for a century or so where feet wore it out. Now it is largely illegible and is placed in the downstream wall.

Opposite it, in the upstream wall, are two large stones which are equally worn: once these bore the coats of arms of Yorkshire and Durham and they mark the county boundary. It was at this spot that the county sheriffs would meet and exchange prisoners. It was also said that if you killed someone in one county and

129

The Road to Rockliffe

Croft Bridge

then rushed past "the blue stane o' th' brigg" you would end up in the jurisdiction of the other and so get away with murder.

In 1745, the Great North Road from Boroughbridge through Northallerton to Darlington and then Durham was turnpiked. This meant that a group of investors paid to maintain the road and charged travellers per mile to use it. A tollhouse was built on the Durham side and a barrier extended across the bridge. Users in carriage or cart or on horse had to pay a toll, which went towards the bridge's maintenance, although there was a small gate which allowed pedestrians to pass for free.

Eight years later, the venerable bridge survived one of the greatest pre-global warming floods, but the tollhouse and £50 of takings was swept away. In 1771, it withstood another great flood which swept through the churchyard and carried off the gates, and drove one old couple up their stairs, onto their roof and then out into the branches of an overhanging tree as the waters rose higher and higher. At length, the old lady told her husband that her arms were exhausted and she could cling no more to the tree. After sad farewells, she dropped into the darkness below.

So devoted was her husband after 40 years of wedded bliss that he thought they

*Above: An old postcard looking down the bank from Hurworth Place to Croft Bridge
Opposite: A 1964 aerial view of Croft Bridge. On the left (Yorkshire) side can be seen the Croft Spa Hotel with an octagonal out-building that was part of its swimming pool. Beside the bridge is St Peter's Church. The right (Durham) side of the bridge is dominated by the field and cricket square of Croft Working Men's Club which was established in a building that used to be the laundry of Hurworth Grange*

131

The Road to Rockliffe

should depart this life together, and he too relinquished his grip.

Imagine his surprise to find, that while sitting in the tree, the waters had receded and he fell through the roof and onto the dry floor of his bedroom beside his wife. And they lived happily ever after...

Until 1795, the bridge was a narrow, single track. Then John Carr, the Surveyor of Bridges in the North Riding, extended it. Carr (1723-1807) was the North of England's foremost architect of his day, obsessed with neatness and symmetry. He was often away from his home in York for a week surveying, so he would buy a large, circular meat pie and, using his compasses, he would divide it exactly into six portions – one for each day of his travels.

He became West Yorkshire's bridgemaster, building major crossings at Sheffield, Rotherham and Ferrybridge, before taking on North Yorkshire's bridges in 1772 for a salary of £100-a-year. He built at least 30 bridges in the riding. One of his earliest was the delightful Greta Bridge, which is a delicate single span with ballustrading. One of his least successful is Aysgarth because it is too tall for most people to see over to the beauty of the tumbling Ure. Perhaps the most appropriate is over the Swale in Richmond. It is deliberately solid and square, so it fits in with the powerful castle behind it.

Beyond bridges, Carr, who was twice Lord Mayor of York, built the church at Rokeby in Teesdale, Northallerton jail and Constable Burton Hall. He built Aske Hall, a grand mansion near Richmond, and Middleton Lodge, which dominates the countryside quite splendidly on the edge of Middleton Tyas.

Plus, in 1795, he widened Croft Bridge by 15ft (five metres) for £3,577 (at the same time he may well also have restored the 14th Century packhorse bridge over Clow

A peculiar postcard view, postmarked 1904, looking north towards County Durham over the parapet of Croft Bridge. The men with the horses and carts appear to be collecting shingle and gravel from the riverbed. It was across here that the Great Blondin was said to have walked on a tightrope in the 1870s

Croft Bridge

Beck at the western edge of Croft). Carr's seven Gothic arches are planted immovably across the Tees – and because his half of the bridge faces upstream, it has had to withstand all the floods, spates, ice floes and debris that the river has flung at it for more than 200 years.

Over the centuries, there have been many great dramas enacted out around the bridge. In 1640, Scottish troops starred in one. They had been overwhelmed by the English up river at Stapleton and fled to Croft where they feared the bridge would be guarded. With their pursuers at their backs, they splashed into the water. Many drowned, but despite their defeat, due to Charles I's weakness that year, the Tees effectively – and briefly – became the border between England and Scotland.

In 1897, great crowds gathered on on the bridge to witness the patriotic unveiling of a brown granite stone near the Yorkshire side which commemorated Queen Victoria's Diamond Jubilee.

But the event that any spectator on the bridge would most want to see unfolding over the parapet was the Great Blondin crossing the Tees on a tightrope. Old timers, whose voices have been silenced by the passing of the years, wrote in a memoir that Blondin tied his rope to a chimney of the Comet hotel on the Durham side and stretched it across to a pole in a "gala field" by Croft Mill, which is now concealed by trees inside the bend in the river. This, they said, took place in the 1870s.

The newspapers of the 1870s are mute on the subject, but they do report that Blondin made his first – and only – appearance in Darlington over the weekend of July 17-29, 1872, 13 years after he had crossed the Niagara Falls. He was the star attraction at a Grand Fete Champetre at Polam Hall, where he performed stunts on a rope tied between two poles.

"The feats that the acrobat performed comprised the astounding acts of walking in a sack, cooking an omelette, carrying a man, riding upon a bicycle, with others of an equally surprising character, all of which were gone through in a manner which fully sustained the reputation of the hero of the Niagara and gave unbounded satisfaction to the spectators," said The Northern Echo.

Blondin put on two shows on the Saturday and two more on the Monday at Polam. So it could be that in his downtime, he nipped to Croft Gala, his palm well greased and his balance steadier than ever, and conquered the mightiest river in the district in front of its venerable bridge.

Or could it be that this story fleshes out an advertisement on the front page of The Northern Echo of April 19,1881. It says that Croft Gala is being held that very day, and that "Bon Bon, the Young Blondin, son of the Original Hero of the Niagara Falls, will give a Grand Performance on the Tight Rope". Whether this really was the Great Blondin's only son, Edward, or some money-making impostor is difficult to tell from this distance, but we can safely assume that he made it safely across because there is no mention in the following day's paper of him making a big splash and taking a tumble. Unless, of course, the whole episode is a figment of the old timers' imagination which appears most likely, on balance...

133

18: Hell's Kettles

ABOUT a mile to the north of Hurworth Place along the old Great North Road are a couple of large puddles. They are protected by a gaggle of geese which, when a stranger approaches, rises from the water like an air force squadron, honking madly from one end and defecating furiously from the other, dropping big cold spladgy bullets as the bombers struggle for take-off.

These puddles are known as Hell's Kettles. They are in a meadow which is part of an area called Oxen-le-fields (the fields by the water), and they are designated a Site of Special Scientific Interest. But how they came to be has perplexed man for the past thousand years.

In 1328, Brompton, the Abbot of Jervaulx, in North Yorkshire, wrote up some historical notes in Latin. Of the year 1179, he remarked: "About Christmas, a wonderful and unheard of event fell out at Oxenhale in the very domain of Lord Hugh, Bishop of Durham. The ground rose up on high with such vehemence that it was equal to the highest tops of the mountains and towered above the lofty pinnacles of the churches; and at that height remained from the ninth hour of the day to sunset. But at sunset it fell with so horrible a crash that it terrified all who saw that heap, and heard the noise of its fall, whence many died from that fear, for the earth swallowed it up, and caused in the same place very deep pits."

What made this event even more terrifying was that it had been foreseen by the ghost of a monk. A few days earlier, the ghost had approached King Henry II, who ruled from 1154 to 1189, and warned him to mend his ways or he would hear "such news as thou shalt mourn to the day of thy death".

Henry laughed off the warning until he heard the news that "at a place called Oxenhale within the Lordship of Darlington the earth was lifted up like a mighty tower and fell with a horrible noise".

What remained after the earth crashed back down again were three pits of water which have fascinated ever since. They emitted an unpleasant aroma, as late as 1634 they were described as "boiling" and yet they are noted for their unnatural stillness. They became famed far and wide as the pools "that from their lothsome brimms do breath a sulphurous sweat, Hell Kettles rightly cald".

Local legend adds colour to their terrible reputation. It says the kettles have no bottoms, and that on a clear day you can see the body of a farmer, eternally swirling, as punishment for blaspheming on St Barnabas' Day (June 11). Henry VIII's inspector is said to have painted a cross on a duck and dropped it in one of the kettles. It was sucked down by the Devil and ended up swimming by Croft Bridge on the nearby Tees.

Then "a man of colour", a diver from the Far East, came to investigate. He took

On a chilly day in 1954, a pair of amazed passers-by point at the swirling body of a farmer trapped in Hell's Kettles in perpetual punishment. Or not, as the case may be

the plunge into Satan's pit, and was drawn along a subterranean passage into the River Skerne.

Strange stuff, although Daniel Defoe was not impressed. Riding by in 1727, he said: "Tis evident they are nothing but old coalpits filled in with water by the Tees."

He was wrong. Today the two remaining Hell's Kettles – the third was filled in when the A167 was widened in the 1950s – are an SSSI due to the rare bog plants and grasses which flourish on their margins.

The larger Double Kettle is filled with dark brown surface water, but the southern Croft Kettle looks very different – greeny-grey – as it is fed from an underground calcareous spring. It forms the only saw-sedge swamp in Durham – more usually found in the fenlands of East Anglia – and its chara hispida (bristly stonewort) and chaetophora pisiformis (green algae) are saved for the nation in the Natural History Museum.

Scientists have studied Hell's Kettles for centuries. They have worked out that they are not unfathomable as the ancients thought because they are 22ft deep, and there are no subterranean passages.

But no one really knows how the pools were created. Mining is unlikely and English Nature merely says that they "originated in 1179 due to natural subsidence".

Or it could be that, due to the dissolute behaviour of the king, the Devil became so emboldened that one day shook the earth so grievously that people died of fright. All that remained to remind – as Abbot Brompton said, "a testimony unto this day" – were pools of a strangely Satanic nature: Hell's Kettles.

19: Sir Ernest Cassel

CROFT House, and its smaller companion, Tees View Villa, are the first signs of life that welcome the visitor to Hurworth Place as he or she travels over the Skerne Bridge from Darlington on the old Great North Road. Hidden by trees and concealed by a high wall, the visitor may pass without noticing them, but they have a fascinating story attached to them of a devious gold-digger, the king's super-rich financier and the mystery of a roll of banknotes left under the pillow of a royal deathbed.

The land on this corner of the Tees' floodplain was bought by Robert Thompson Maxwell on July 1, 1856. His background is unclear – he was born in Stockton, had lived in Saltburn and was either a pawnbroker or a master mariner – but on his new piece of floodplain, he built Croft House between 1861 and 1865. It had a delightful aspect over the Tees, but a noisy rear outlook into the railway coal depot and gas works. There he retired with his second wife, Annie, whom he had married in 1851 and was "many years younger than her husband". Their three children, Arthur, Annette and Ernest, grew up there.

Robert died in Croft House on June 28, 1871, of gastric fever, a week after making a new will. He wrote his three sons from his first marriage out of it and left his estate – valued at up to £30,000 (about £2.6 million today) – to Annie and their three children. Immediately, the three Maxwell brothers launched a law suit claiming that

Croft House, built in the early 1860s, was the setting for Maxwell versus Maxwell

their father's "mental faculties were so impaired by the disease...that he could not understand" his new will.

Within six months of her husband's death, Annie remarried a French gentleman, Eugene Du Boison. He was a "traveller in Roman Catholic vestments", a job which had taken him to Scotland, France and America. Peculiarly, he also went by the alias of Eugene Adrian Marchand – in that name he taken charge of the burial of two children, presumably his own, in St Pancras, London, in 1870.

The family soon rumbled that Du Boison was a gold-digger and in 1874 the marriage was dissolved in the High Court in London. Du Boison was arrested for the seventh time for making false declarations in his attempt to gain an English naturalisation certificate, but still he launched a counterclaim. Du Boison versus Maxwell and the will dispute, Maxwell versus Maxwell, drifted through the London courts until Annie died in 1879. The cases had drained her estate. She had had to remortgage Croft House for £4,000 to pay her London solicitor, and her eldest son, Arthur, seems to have fled to the Channel Islands to escape liability.

All Annie could leave her three children was a large unpaid mortgage. But her daughter, Annette, had married the richest man in the kingdom: Sir Ernest Cassel.

Cassel was born in 1852 in Cologne, the son of a modest Jewish banker. He left school at 14 destined for a drab business career. Instead, aged 18, he arrived in Liverpool carrying only a bundle of clothes and a violin.

Immediately he made his mark in the world of high finance, and within five years was earning £5,000 a year (nearly £430,000 in today's values) in London bank-rolling American railways.

His hobbies were horses, hunting and shooting. Perhaps it was this that drew him towards Darlington which offered some of the best hunting territory in the country. For a while in the 1870s, he rented Walworth Castle and perhaps during a Zetland Hunt meet, he met Annette. They married at Westminster Register Office on September 3, 1878 – the day that Cassel became a naturalised British subject.

By this time, he had £150,000 in his bank account and he had a finger in every conceivable pie. His biggest assets were in Sweden where he bankrolled iron ore

Sir Ernest Cassel (1852-1921), a merchant banker and capitalist, arrived penniless in Britain as a 18-year-old but became one of the wealthiest men in the country and a close friend of the king. Croft House was the family home of his wife, Annette

It is said that Cassel himself created the curious Tees View Cottages

mines, railways, docks, ships, etc. Therefore, when his debt-laden mother-in-law died, he was able to finesse the Maxwells' money problems away. Arthur returned from the Channel Islands to take up residence in Croft House, and it is believed that Tees View Villa was built beside it for another family member.

Village folklore suggests that Cassel himself converted the groom's quarters into the spectacular oddities that are Tees View Cottages. The castellated cottages are covered with embellishments of unicorns and lions. This sounds as unlikely as the cottages' appearance because Cassel was a humourless man. Yet he later improved his Park Lane home so that there were 800 tons of marble spread throughout its six kitchens, there was an oak-panelled dining room to seat 100, and there was a distinctive entrance hall panelled in lapis lazuli and green-veined cream marble. Perhaps Croft House was the beginning of his interest in eccentric design.

On December 18, 1880, Annette bore Ernest a daughter, Amalia Mary Maud, in Kensington, but the next year the young mother contracted tuberculosis. As she lay on her deathbed on September 15, 1881, she told her beloved Ernest that she feared she would never see him again because she was a Roman Catholic and he was a Jew. At her behest, the priest who had been summoned to give her the last rites instead baptised him in her bedroom. She died happy and his secret conversion did not become public until 20 years later when he was sworn on to the Privy Council.

Cassel was devoted to Annette, and never had an intimate relationship again. Instead, he doted on his daughter and immersed himself in his business. He organised huge loans for the governments of Mexico, China and Uruguay; he rebuilt the Egyptian economy and financed the Nile dam, still regarded as one of the greatest civil engineering feats; his money was responsible for building railways the length of North America; he financed the Central Line of the London Underground...

In business he was a loner. He sat on no company boards, he had no directorships, he took no partners. He was not an entrepreneur, nor a banker. He was a fixer. He put his success down to "hard work, good information and then instinct".

In 1896, in the paddock at Newmarket, he met the Prince of Wales – whom he looked uncannily like. "A genuine and warm attachment grew up between these two men of such dissimilar temperament, to the puzzlement of those around the court," writes Anthony Allfrey in his 1991 book, Edward VII and His Jewish Court.

He took charge of the Prince of Wales' finances, and when Edward succeeded Victoria, Cassel found himself the most important financier of his era. His nickname at court was "Windsor Cassel". When Maud had a daughter in 1901, the king became her godfather and she was called Edwina after him.

In May 1910, when the Edward VII fell ill, he called from his deathbed for two people: his favourite mistress, Mrs Alice Keppel (whose fortune Cassel managed) and Sir Ernest himself. Cassel rushed from Egypt, on a chartered steamer, with Maud, who was also ailing.

When he reached London, the king told him: "I am very seedy, but I wanted to see you." Cassel was Edward's last visitor. The monarch was found dead next morning with an envelope stuffed with a fortune in banknotes on his pillow. No one understands why.

King Edward VII

In the same year, Cassel retired from active business. Then Maud, his daughter, died aged 33 of tuberculosis despite Cassel's best nursing attentions. He became a sad and lonely man, shifting unhappily between homes across continental Europe, his only joy being his grand-daughter Edwina who lived with him when he was in Park Lane.

But worse was to come, because Cassel was a German and a Jew. He was very closely acquainted with the financiers who were paying for the Kaiser's growing war machine. With Winston Churchill, he tried desperately to head off the inevitable war, but found himself vilified in the Press for his enemy roots. An unfortunate coincidence was that his horse, named Hapsburg just like the Kaiser, came second in the 1914 Derby.

In May 1915, he felt forced to make a public protestation of his "unfailing loyalty

The Road to Rockliffe

and devotion to this country". But he was shunned by his former friends, lived in isolation in Bournemouth, and in August 1918 was the subject of a heated debate in the House of Lords, where it was demanded that this German Jew be evicted from the Privy Council.

He was not, and once the war was over, he donated £1m (over £42m today) to George V's rebuilding plans. Half of it was spent on higher education, including the creation of the Workers' Education Association, and the other half on helping the mentally handicapped.

Then Cassel's health began to fail. Like Edward VII, he was overweight and too fond of cigars. His doctors felt that the smog of winter London was likely to be too much for him, so he bought an £88,000 estate in Belgium in preparation for a healthy retreat.

In 1920, Cassel held a lavish debutante's ball for Edwina in Park Lane and she met Queen Victoria's great-grandson, Lord Louis Mountbatten. In September 1921, the two youngsters were ensconced in a Scottish castle, Mountbatten awaiting the right romantic moment to propose. It never came as news arrived informing him that his father, Prince Louis of Battenberg, had died, so the pair rushed to London. There Edwina learned that her grandfather, Sir Ernest Cassel, had died the night before.

The financier had cancelled a dinner party he had been hosting for the Liberal leader HH Asquith and his wife. He retreated to his room where his footman found him dead at his desk, his head slumped into his papers.

Churchill sent a long letter to Edwina. "Your grandfather was a great man and he made a mark on his generation and on the world which will last long," he said. "The last talk we had, he told me that he hoped he would live to see me at the head of affairs. I have lost a good friend whose like I shall never see again."

Sir Ernest Cassel left a fortune of £7.3m – that would be worth £250m today, one of the largest ever amassed in a lifetime in this country. He also gave at least £2m away. But he said: "You know, money does not make for happiness." He rejected his German and Jewish backgrounds, but was never fully accepted in his chosen English world. His brusque manner meant he made few friendships – except with Edward, which according to Allfrey was "the only real pleasure, amounting almost to happiness, that his wealth bought him".

Personal happiness lasted three brief years with his marriage to Annette of Hurworth Place, and he was particularly bitter at his daughter's early death. He said: "I have had everything in the world that I did not want, and nothing that I did."

Had he lived a little longer, he would doubtlessly have been overjoyed to see Edwina marry Mountbatten in 1922 – although Mountbatten's life would end horrifically at the hands of the IRA in 1979.

With Cassel's death, the family's connection with their corner of the Tees floodplain came to an end: Croft House was auctioned in 1923. For much of the 20th Century, it was in the hands of the wine merchanting branch of the Pease family, but even they didn't have the wealth of the king's financier.

20: Comet

COMET was a superstar of its day. It was an oversized, interbred freak, but it sparkled like no other because it was bigger than every other. Two hundred years after its death, a pub on the road to Rockliffe is still named after it, and its gargantuan inspiration can be found in the works of Lewis Carroll who lived next door to his creator.

Comet was a product of its age: an age of urbanisation and turnipisation. Times were changing fast as Britons were leaving the countryside to work in the new industrial factories and to live in the new industrial towns. Agriculture had to adapt. It had to grow more food with fewer labourers. It was helped by the arrival of the turnip.

In pre-turnip times, farmers found it too expensive to feed large numbers of cattle over winter, so at Martinmas (November 11) there was an annual slaughter. Only animals selected for breeding were kept, and the rest became meat, salted to store. In 1730, Charles "Turnip" Townshend, an East Anglian politician obsessed by root vegetables, introduced his cattle to the Dutch turnip. They loved it. This meant cattle could now be fed cheaply over winter.

Post-turnip, with the annual Martinmas slaughter a thing of the past, farmers started breeding to refine their beasts so that they lived longer and grew into hefty animals, full of meat and tallow (fat) to make candles.

In 1779, Christopher Hill, of Blackwell, on the southern outskirts of Darlington, slaughtered the six-year-old Blackwell Ox. It weighed 152 stone (935kg) and caused

The Comet pub, on the right of this late 19th Century picture

The Road to Rockliffe

The famous Comet bull whose name lives on in Hurworth Place

a sensation – it was the first ox to have its picture painted and distributed as a souvenir print in the manner that today a popstar hands out signed photos to their fans.

The sensation sparked a craze. Farmers across south Durham competed to breed the biggest beasts. At Ketton, to the north of Darlington, the Colling brothers, Robert and Charles, interbred the best local animals to create their ideal bull or cow: an animal that fattened quickly, had a thick carcass of beef, but didn't lose the ability to produce milk – elsewhere in the country, farmers created incestual freaks which were vastly fat but were unable to produce milk or, for that matter, to stand up without the aid of supportive poles.

The Colling brothers' first superstar was the Ketton Ox which they exhibited on Darlington market in 1799 where because of its great bulk – it weighed 214 stone (1,360kg) – it caused a great stir.

They sold it two years later for a profitable £140 (about £8,000 today), and it ended in the hands of John Day of Rotherham. He renamed it the Durham Ox and turned it into a lucrative travelling freakshow. The monster embarked on a six-year tour which took it the length and breadth of the country, pulled in a specially-constructed, padded carriage by four or six horses, depending on the state of the road. It spent most of 1802 starring in London where takings in a single day were £97.

The Durham Ox was a good looking, well-natured thing – "my wife who rode with him in the carriage found him harmless as a fawn and familiar as a lapdog", wrote Mr Day in his memoirs – which was surprisingly agile for one so large. Merchandise, such as prints, china plates and scale models, were produced of it as Mr Day milked his ox, and many of the communities that it visited were so impressed that they named a pub after it.

The end for the Durham Ox began on February 19, 1807. Having travelled more than 3,000 miles in six years, it arrived for a gig in Oxford. As it manoeuvred its bulk out of its carriage, it slipped, dislocating a hip. After eight weeks, it showed no sign of recovery. It was in pain and Mr Day, to his credit, called in the butchers – three of them – to slaughter it.

Despite having lost weight during its two months of ill health, the monster weighed 271 stone (1,724kg) when it died.

Back in Ketton, the Collings continued to breed. The Durham Ox's half-sister was The White Heifer. In 1800, aged four, it weighed 164 stone (1,043kg), and it was exhibited at Three Kings Hotel, in Piccadilly, London, which billed it as "the greatest wonder in the world of the kind". The Colling brothers became so famous that King George III leased one of their bulls for three years to improve his herd in Windsor.

Comet, born in 1804, was the Collings' biggest bull. It was, quite literally, outstanding in its field. "He had a fine masculine head, broad and deep chest, shoulders well laid back, crops and loins good, hind quarters, long, straight and well-packed, thighs thick, breast full and well let-down, with nice straight hocks and hind legs," enthused Charles Colling. "He had fair-sized horns, ears straight and hairy, and a grandeur of style and carriage that baffled description."

An indication of the Collings' inbreeding programme is that Comet had the same father and grandfather – a bull called Favourite, who was mated with its mother and its own daughter born by its own mother. A cow called Phoenix was both of Comet's grandmothers.

In 1810, Charles, 60, retired. His sale of animals at Ketton Hall attracted crowds from all over the North. Comet was the star attraction and was sold for £1,000 – the

The Colling brothers, Robert and Charles, who bred Comet. In 1810, Charles retired to Monkend Hall, Croft-on-Tees, where he died in 1836

The Road to Rockliffe

Monkend Hall in Croft-on-Tees was the home of Charles Colling, the breeder of Comet

first thousand pound ox, making it as much of a celebrated landmark as the first million pound footballer. It might have made more as Sir Henry Vane Tempest rode up minutes after the hammer had come down and offered the new owners £1,600 cash. They refused, and took Comet off to Cleasby in the hope that it would transfer its genes around their stud.

Charles made £7,115 17s by selling his 47 animals. "Well, we've beaten all England in prices and have no shorthorns left," his wife said, sadly, and they retired to Monkend Hall, in Croft. Charles died there on January 16, 1836, aged 85, and his wife lived until 1850. From 1843, her neighbours at The Rectory were the Dodgsons and their 11-year-old son, Charles. The story of Mrs C's vast bovine wonder inspired the youngster to call one of his family magazines The Comet and, in later life, as Lewis Carroll, he would become famous for his fanciful distortions of nature.

And there was little more distorted than Comet. It died in Cleasby in 1815, and many of its ginormous remains are in Darlington museum. One rib was despatched to the Royal Shorthorn Society in Warwickshire and another, measuring 2ft 1ins (62cms) long was sent to California for the Americans to marvel at. Even in the land of the supersize burger, they had seen nothing as extra large as the superstar Comet.

The Comet pub, on the road to Rockliffe, served the travellers on the Great North Road as they came over Croft Bridge. It had competition, as the Pig and Whistle pub stood opposite with a blacksmith's forge attached until road-widening in the 1930s.

The Comet's next generations of clientele came with the branchline that created a coal depot behind it, but its greatest prosperity came in the mainline era when Croft Spa was a honeypot. Like a Spanish resort around a sandy Mediterranean cala, buildings quickly sprung up to service the tourists. The mainline station opened on March 3, 1841 (see Chapter 4) and soon the riverside around The Comet was filled

Comet

The Comet is hidden from view by the terrace known as Tees View on the left, but behind the telegraph pole can be seen the old Pig and Whistle and the smithy. Right: The Station Hotel on the bank was another hostelry serving the tourists

by cafes and the hillside behind it was populated by shops to pop into and places to stay. There was the Station Hotel, with, at the top of the bank, a two-sided square of lodging houses in Banks Terrace, plus you can still make out the grand entrance portico of a Temperance Hotel.

Previous generations were remarkably inexact in their terminology for this new touristy town. Today, in an age of postcodes and sat-navs, Croft-on-Tees ends precisely with Yorkshire at the River Tees. Over the bridge and you enter County Durham and the village of Hurworth Place which acts as the hors d'oeuvres to Hurworth itself. But in the past, when maps were just rough squiggles, Croft spilled over the river and ran roughshod over Hurworth Place. It didn't come to an end until beyond Pilmore where it met the boundary of Hurworth, and so Alfred Backhouse often gave his address as Croft when he was quite clearly elsewhere. And so, the mainline railway station that bore the name of the North Yorkshire village of Croft was actually in the County Durham settlement of Hurworth Place.

None of which mattered to the tourists. They were quite happy to send postcards home from wherever they were staying...

The Road to Rockliffe

Edwardian picture postcards looking down the bank at Croft Spa – although we today would call it Hurworth Place as it is over the river in County Durham

Comet

Postcards of Hurworth Road – the road that leads to Rockliffe – show how its shops and cafes thrived on the tourist trade of the early 20th Century. On the right of the card below is the village hall built by Elizabeth Backhouse of Hurworth Grange

147

21: Old Hurworth

'ONCE, on some spring or summer morning," wrote Edith Harper in 1908, barely pausing for breath as she dashed from one village to the next, "you have wended your way down the Hurworth lane, from Croft station, with the plantations of Rockliffe Park on your right hand, the trim hawthorn hedges of Hurworth Grange like a green wall on your left, and have come in sight of a cluster of bright red roofs nestling among fields and meadows at the foot of the lane, with the Cleveland Hills and old Roseberry Topping for a dim blue background, and the varied foliage of elm and oak, chestnut and maple, making an enchanting pageant everywhere...you lose yourself in an artist's ecstasy over the sylvan beauties of the 'wood by the water'."

Welcome to Hurworth – the wood by the water. Not all philologists agree that it is the "wood by the water". Dissenters point out that down the centuries it has been known as Hurdevordo, Hurthewoth, Hurthworthe or Hortheworthe, which all translate as "the clearing of the wood". Both of these derivations rely on the ancient word "hurst", meaning wood, being found at the start of Hurworth. If the word at the beginning is "hurthe", meaning a herdsman, then we have a settlement that grew up around an animal-keeper's croft. Or if it is "hurth", then we have an enclosure made of hurdles...

Whatever. "Hurworth is a beautiful village scattered along a steep bank above the Tees and commanding a rich, though bounded, landscape southwards extending over a fertile plain washed by a gallant sweep of the river: the swift rise of the Yorkshire grounds closes the prospect," wrote the Durham historian Robert Surtees in 1823 of the village where his kinsman, Thomas Surtees Raine, was buying land in the river's eastern loop.

Hurworth is an ancient place, first mentioned in history in connection with an unusual medical malady. Legend tells how St Godric, who died at Finchale Abbey near Durham City in 1170, once healed "a matron of Hurdevorde named Bricteva suffering from flying gout".

Other snippets go back further than even Bricteva's curious complaint. As you walk east down the road from Rockliffe, as Edith Harper described in 1908, you come to the crossroads which was once the heart of old Hurworth. On the left is the village shop, on the right is Blind Lane which leads down to the Tees via Cross Bank and the Ring Field. On Cross Bank was found a fragment of a 9th Century Saxon stone cross covered with "crisp and confident" carving. It is now in Durham Cathedral. Crosses were quite common in Durham villages in Saxon times, but Hurworth's fragment is unique in the county: it is a foot-long section of the base, and bases rarely survive.

When it was new, it was part of a settlement which included a Saxon manor house,

Old Hurworth

a chapel and a parsonage. The old school, which opened on June 12, 1829, on the Blind Lane crossroads was built on "Chapel Green", and now all that is left of the Saxon settlement is the nearby Old Parsonage. It has "1450" over its door – but the door itself, studded with nails, may be even older as it is said to have come from the old chapel.

In the parsonage, the parson would sit at the top of his grand staircase receiving the villagers' tithes which he stored in the tithe barn behind. This ancient building was pulled down in 1879 and the 13th Century timbers from its roof were turned into choirstalls for the "new" church.

The "new" church, All Saints at the eastern edge of the village green, has a Norman beginning so it is nearly a thousand years old. It started as a squat riverside church but has been re-built so many times that only six pillars in the nave and a bit of the belltower have survived from those earliest days. Indeed, Thomas Surtees Raine, of Pilmore Grange, may well have paid for the 1831 rebuild, and the vicar, the Reverend Robert Hopper Williamson, paid for the most recent, in 1871. The coats of arms of both the vicar and Surtees Raine can be found on the church, although

Above: A painting of All Saints Church, Hurworth, before it was substantially rebuilt in 1871. The church seems to sit on a hillock with the River Tees on the right
Right: An 1899 drawing of Hurworth's unusual Saxon cross base which is now in Durham Cathedral

The Road to Rockliffe

pride of place goes to the four ancient arms on the tower. They belong to the Neville, Tailboys (or Tailbois), Dacre and Greystock families who ruled the district in the most distant of days.

Inside the church lie two recumbent knights from those families, sleeping in stone. One, in Frosterley marble, is an effigy of Lord Dacre, the 12th Century founder of Neasham Abbey. He sleeps with his visor down and sword unsheathed, as if he's ready to do battle. Next to him lies Ralph Fitz-William, the 1st Lord of Grimthorpe and the 1st Lord of Greystock, with his head on two pillows. He was a "distinguished soldier" who was with Edward I at the Siege of Caerlaverock Castle, near Dumfries, in 1300 and who, in 1313, received a pardon from Edward II for his part in the death of the king's favourite, Piers Gaveston.

Ralph died in 1316 and was originally buried with Lord Dacre in Neasham Priory, of which he was patron. Following Henry VIII's dissolution of the monasteries, the priory was robbed and the two knights slowly made their way up to All Saints, stopping in various gardens along the way where they acted as ornaments.

Of the Tailboys, we know that six generations were lords of the manor at Hurworth, including Gilbert Lord Tailboys whose wife, Elizabeth, was lady-in-waiting to Catherine of Aragon, Henry VIII's first wife. Elizabeth did more than just wait. In 1519 she gave birth to a son who was not a Tailboys. Henry VIII recognised the boy as his own, and called him Henry FitzRoy, Duke of Richmond. For a while, as the king ran through wives in his desperate search for a male heir, it seemed Elizabeth's illegitimate son might become king of England. This prospect ended when the prince died of consumption at the age of 17.

Gilbert's legitimate son, Robert Lord Tailboys, became heir to the manor of

Looking east in Hurworth with the Bay Horse on the left and the church on the right

Hurworth, but he died in 1532 without children and so there were no Tailboys left to inherit. Their estate was split up and sold off, which meant large parcels of land were available – like that inside a certain loop of the Tees – to anyone who had the means to buy.

"While the village is the permanent residence of several respectable families, the salubrity of its situation and the beauty of its scenery are very attractive to visitors," wrote historian William Fordyce in 1857, when Alfred Backhouse was starting to show an interest in purchasing Pilmore. Fordyce's pronouncement may well still be true today, but Hurworth's past has not always been salubrious.

The plague hit hard in 1645. "The Lord struck three-and-forty people here in this month of July, near all in this town, viz Hurworth," say old documents. Other versions of the story put the death count much higher, with all but 75 of the village's 750 inhabitants wiped out.

The Reverend Thomas Thompson recorded the names of his parishioners as they succumbed to the disease. At first, the rector's handwriting was strong and legible, but with each successive name it became weaker and spidery until it just tailed away.

The final entry was in a new, firm hand – possibly that of the vicar of Eryholme. It recorded the death and burial of Mr Thompson.

As death does not discriminate, the rector must have been buried with his parishioners in the plague pits beneath Hurworth's most attractive feature: the wide, undulating village green on which the Scouts hold their Strawberry Fair every summer. It is said that because the dead were brought from miles around by the river – from Neasham, Eryholme, Dalton and possibly even Pilmore – up to 1,500 plague victims were buried beneath the green.

The arched door, with a sundial above, belong to the Bay Horse in Hurworth

151

The Road to Rockliffe

The lone boatman would come ashore at the foot of Knellgate and haul his grisly cargo up the dank lane that still leads onto the green. Then he would ring a bell – possibly in All Saints church; possibly in the tower of the large house, Dovercourt, beside Knellgate. This deathknell would warn the living to stay inside to avoid contamination and to alert the gravedigger to his morbid duty.

For fear of infection, the gravedigger would also work alone. His task began in Limeyard, next to the Bay Horse Inn, where he would fill his barrow with quicklime and wheel it over to the green. There he would enlarge the pit, remove the body from the coffin, lay it in the hole on a bed of shavings and cover it with lime to aid decomposition. A layer of topsoil would complete the job, and the communally-owned coffin – too expensive a piece of apparatus to waste on a single underground usage – would await its next unfortunate inhabitant.

And so the bodies on Hurworth's gruesome green lie ten deep in three mass graves. As they decay, the grass gently settles into picturesque undulations, occasionally giving up a part of a skeleton to remind the living of the fate of the dead.

Despite all this, Hurworth Green is a desireable address, edged with grand houses. One of the most grand was Hurworth House, home for the second half of the 19th Century to Colonel George Scurfield, the leading villager who was, according to his obituary in the Darlington and Stockton Times, "a man of exceedingly high culture and brilliance".

He was born on February 4, 1810, the second son of William Grey of Norton, but assumed his mother's maiden name of Scurfield by Royal licence – presumably because there was a lucrative inheritance attached to it.

Looking east as the boys play cricket on the undulations of the plague pits

Old Hurworth

He was educated at St John's College, Cambridge, and moved to Hurworth when he married Anne Alice Williamson, the daughter of the church-rebuilder, the Reverend Robert Hopper-Williamson. He was chairman of the Durham county bench of magistrates and involved in good works and important committees across the North-East. He was best-known for founding the Volunteers Movement of part-time soldiers (something akin to today's Territorial Army) in Darlington. For four years, he was Honorary Colonel of the 1st Volunteer Batallion, the Durham Light Infantry, and as a Conservative-inclined military Anglican, he was a regular opponent of the Liberal-minded pacifist Quakers led by the Peases and the Backhouses.

Under the Colonel, Hurworth House must have been palatial. Features highlighted when it was auctioned in 1948 include a "cosy smoke room" next to the Gun Room, a flight of stairs leading to "The Nook or Tea Landing, a lofty apartment with large Gothic windows from which access is obtained to the Strong Room", plus the "Handsome and Well-Proportioned Drawing Room, with a Fine Mahogany Mantlepiece and old Biblical Scenes in Blue Tiled Jambs, white shell pattern Carved China shelves in recess, and a Beautiful Gilt Mirror with fluted sides resting on a coloured marble table with Scurfield Arms inlaid".

But the pride of the property was the "Secluded and Beautiful Tees-side Pleasure Grounds" which dropped 50ft down to the river. Water continuously trickled down through stone troughs and manmade courses, passed an icehouse dug into the bank, and onto the boathouse and jetty, which was made from stone sleepers laid for the Stockton and Darlington Railway in 1825. Next to the boathouse was an Engine

Looking west in Hurworth with the spire of the old school on the left

The Road to Rockliffe

Top: An old postcard view of the crossroads at the centre of old Hurworth before the Scurfield Monument was built in 1911
Bottom: The first school in Hurworth was opened in 1770 in what is now the garage of the Dovercourt house overlooking the Green. On June 12, 1829, a new school was opened on the old crossroads. The Scurfield drinking fountain was built in front of it

House fitted with a gas engine that pumped water up to the tower, which can still be seen on the highest part of the green, so that the flow was never-ending.

The Colonel died on Boxing Day, 1895, and his obituary concludes: "Only those who had the privilege of knowing him intimately can realise the extent of the loss of one who represented a class which seems to be disappearing from our midst – uniting as he did the courtesy and chivalry of the ancien regime with the advanced thought of the latter half of the 19th Century."

His lasting memorial is the churchyard lych-gate, built in 1898, but his daughter, Alice Joanna Sarah Dorothea Scurfield, has the Scurfield Monument in her memory. Alice took on her father's leading village role, and her time coincided with the arrival of mains water and the closure of the village's handpumps. The villagers were rather attached to their pumps and when in 1895 the sanitary inspector condemned the one beside All Saints as "exceedingly foul and unfit for drinking...the close proximity of the churchyard to the pump might account for the pollution", they clubbed together and raised enough money to send a sample to an independent analyst.

Unfortunately, in their alacrity, they sent the sample to the same sanitary inspector, who came to the same insanitary conclusion.

The last pump closed in October 1909. It was near the site of the Saxon manor house. In 1911, Alice told the local council that "since the pump was removed, the animals in Hurworth, and those passing through, have suffered great privations" because of lack of water. A drinking fountain was the answer, said Alice, and she badgered the council into paying £5 a year to the water company once the village had paid for the construction.

Hurworth House, once the home of Colonel George Scurfield

And so the Scurfield Monument was erected on the site of the last pump in time for George V's coronation in 1911. When Alice died two years later, she left an estate worth £34,000, which included £100 to be invested in bonds returning five per cent a year to cover the cost of the water.

Although the fountain has not had a water supply for nearly 50 years now, it still stands on the crossroads that were once at the heart of old Hurworth, welcoming visitors to the salubrious settlement.

"Hurworth irresistibly suggests a village in one of Jane Austen's novels," concluded Edith Harper in 1908, which is a truth almost universally acknowledged.

22: William Emerson

"Beware of the man who will not engage in idle conversation; he is planning to steal your walking stick or water your stock." **William Emerson (1701-82) of Hurworth**

"WHEN I was young," said Thomas Jefferson, the third President of the United States, "mathematics was the passion of my life." And that was because when he was at college, he was introduced to the joys of sums by The Doctrine of Fluxions, a textbook written by Hurworth's most famous son. William Emerson was known for his prodigious in-take of ale, and for his curmudgeonly manner and vulgar tongue, but he was renowned as a mathematician. His textbooks taught generations of Georgian scholars, and American presidents, how to do arithmetic, calculus, algebra, trigonometry, geometry and astronomy.

Yet when Emerson was a boy, he was regarded as "cloddish". He was born in Hurworth where his father, Dudley, was the schoolmaster. So cloddish was he that he was sent away to schools in Newcastle and York. It didn't work. He returned in 1730 and tried to run his late father's school. However, Emerson was an impatient teacher with a terrible temper. His pupils left and the school closed in 1733.

Emerson resolved to live on the £60-or-so a year that his father's estate at Castle Gate, near Eastgate, in Weardale, brought in.

In 1735, he married Elizabeth, the daughter of the Reverend Dr John Johnson, the rector of Hurworth. The rector had offered a £500 dowry with his daughter's hand, but he disapproved of her choice. He treated his scruffy son-in-law with contempt and refused to pay, so Emerson loaded all his wife's clothes in a barrow and wheeled it round to the parsonage, saying he refused "to be beholden to such a fellow for a single rag". He also vowed to prove the rector wrong.

Each summer, he retreated to Castle Gate to work on his books. As a mathematician, Emerson didn't break new ground, but his brilliantly-ordered mind saw the complex processes far clearer than anyone else. Similarly, he was regarded as a poor musician – he invented a violin with two first strings – but he was in great demand locally to tune harpsichords because his ear could hear more clearly than anyone else's.

Aged 42, he published his first book, The Doctrine of Fluxions (fluxions being what today we call calculus). It immediately became a best-seller. Said Emerson immodestly: "I stepped forth, like a giant in all his might."

He followed it up with The Projection of the Sphere, Orthographic, Stereographic and Gnomical, although the work that really sealed his reputation was The Principles of Mechanics of 1754. This was still being reprinted for students in the 1830s, long after his death.

William Emerson

The Bay Horse in Hurworth, which has a sundial above its arched doors, was only a couple of hundred yards from the home of William Emerson (right). Emerson's house was to the left of this picture and was demolished in the 1960s

Before committing to print, Emerson tested every one of the theories in his books. In Mechanics, for example, there is a drawing of an elaborate sewing machine which Emerson made for his wife. When researching A Treatise of Navigation, he had his young helpers splashing about in the Tees, building boats. The "whole crew got swampt frequently", he reported. The Mathematical Principles of Geography was published in 1770 and was accompanied by a work entitled Dialling, or the Art of Drawing Dials. This was based on the 30 sundials Emerson had erected on house walls all over Hurworth. Unfortunately, only one authenticated Emerson dial remains: on the Bay Horse pub, shaped like a pair of protractors.

As well as his books, Emerson wrote strident scientific articles for magazines. These often appeared under pen names: Merones, which is in the stained glass of the Emerson Arms pub in Hurworth, was a scramble of his surname; Philofluentimechanalgegeomastrolongo, though, is a little more difficult to explain.

Three sundials from William Emerson's heyday remain in Hurworth. The dial on the Bay Horse (left) is dated 1793. The dial overlooking the Green (centre) says Hurworth's latitude is 51 degrees and 34 minutes whereas the 1772 round dial (right), by his pupil John Hunter which is on West End, says 54.34. Modern computations suggest that Hurworth's latitude is 54.48

In many of his experiments he was assisted by his friend John Hunter. One day, a carriageload of mathematical professors from Cambridge University arrived at his door on Hurworth Green with a problem they were unable to solve. Emerson cast an eye over it and called Hunter down from the roof, where he was fixing tiles, and told him to answer it. After a few moments, Hunter handed over his hat with the solution chalked on the crown. "Quite correct," said Emerson, handing the hat to the professors.

The university types didn't understand how the solution had been arrived at, so Emerson said: "Take the hat with ye, and return it when you've discovered the explanation."

As the dispenser of such wisdom, Emerson was widely consulted. Edward Montagu, brother of the Duke of Manchester, came to walk the Hurworth fields with him, deep in mathematical discussion.

The Royal Society wished to make him a Fellow, but he refused, saying: "When a man becomes eminent, he has to pay quarterly for it. This is the way ingenuity is rewarded in England. Damn them and their FRS too."

Villagers held such a man in awe, especially as he was able to predict – possibly even control – the patterns of the stars and the appearance of comets.

One Sunday, churchgoers were astonished to see a young boy transfixed in the top of Emerson's tree as if a spell had been cast on him. A villager asked Emerson if he could help with the return of the washing which had been stolen from her line, and Emerson let it be known that he would cast another spell trapping the culprit at the top of the church cherry tree unless the apparel was reunited with its rightful owner.

Over night it was, and Emerson had no need to cast the second spell. Which was just as well, as the first spell consisted of him standing, invisible to the churchgoers, at the foot of his apple tree, armed with an axe and threatening to "hag the legs off" the young scrumper if he dared to come down from the branches.

This vulgar language was typical of Emerson, as was the coarseness of his dress. His wife Elizabeth spun and bleached the linen (Hurworth, with its subterranean rooms tumbling down to the Tees, once had more than 150 residents who were weavers) which she then turned into his clothes on her elaborate sewing machine. He always buttoned the top and bottom of his coat but left the middle open and billowing. To keep his chest warm, he wore his shirt back to front.

He was also renowned for inventing shin-covers: pieces of sacking tied above the knee with string. Shin-covers allowed him to sit in his favourite chair as close to the fire as possible without his protruding lower legs getting burnt.

The Victorian historian William Longstaffe wrote: "His wigs were made of brown or a dirty flaxen coloured hair, which at first appeared bushy and tortuous behind, but which grew pendulous through age, till at length it became quite straight, having probably never undergone the operation of the comb." However, because Emerson habitually slid his hand beneath his wig at the rear of his head, it distinctively sagged at the back.

He walked everywhere – even down to London, carrying his manuscripts. When Mr Montagu offered him the use of a carriage, he replied: "Damn your whim-wham! I had rather walk."

Most weeks he walked into Darlington to buy his provisions at the Monday market, leading a horse which would carry them home. Only Monday turned into

All Saints Church, Hurworth, where William Emerson is buried

The Road to Rockliffe

The tomb chest of William Emerson. John Hunter lies just behind him

Tuesday which turned into Wednesday as Emerson fell into idle conversation in the pubs around the market place.

"It is remarkable that his ale didn't injure his appetite, and that he never felt a head-ache or any ill effects afterwards," marvelled Longstaffe.

In later life, it caught up with him. He would stand for hours in the Tees, indulging in his hobby of fishing and hoping that the water would wash the gout out of him. Towards the end of his life, he was greatly troubled by gallstones, shouting out his wish that "my soul might have shaken off its rags of mortality without such a clitter-my-clatter".

He died on May 21, 1782, aged 81, and left specific instructions for the wording on his headstone. This stone was damaged during rebuilding of the church in 1832, and in 1860 the villagers clubbed together to replace it with the impressive chest which is just beneath the tower, within sight of Colonel George Skelly of Seringapatam.

They copied the words from the old to the new – although the new is now so old that its weathered words are once more hard to make out. The top line is in Hebrew, which Emerson chose because it used his favourite insult – to him, everybody was a "damned fule" – and because it spoke of the universality of death: "Then said I in my heart, as it happeneth to the fool, so it happeneth even to me."

The inscription beneath is in Latin which the ol' big head must have written himself: "Underneath are interred the mortal remains of William Emerson, whose merit and science remained long unnoticed, although in him were united the virtues of simplicity and perfect integrity, with uncommon genius. That he was a great mathematician, if you have read his works, this stone need not inform you; if not, read them and learn."

23: Drink

THE most imposing of all the monuments in All Saints' churchyard was put up in 1861 by the Hurworth Temperance Society. Ironically, within a drunkard's stagger there is an older gravestone dated May 25, 1838. It is dedicated to the memory of Robert Hodgson, aged 89, an innkeeper. Despite Mr Hodgson's longevity, Hurworth was especially fervent in its espousal of the temperance cause. Besides the churchyard monument, two substantial buildings remain in the village from those non-drinking days.

The earliest temperance driving force in Hurworth was a fiercesome matriach, Mrs Margaret Maynard, whose name appears first and foremost on the All Saints monument. Mrs Maynard was a Methodist, but not of the sedate variety who had established their Wesleyan chapel in the west end in May 1827 (it was enlarged in 1865 and rebuilt 1954). She was a "Ranter" – an evangelical Primitive Methodist. She composed a rhyming couplet advising young girls how to maintain their honour:

*"If a maid would keep a good name
She would bide at home as if she was lame."*

Mrs Maynard's Primitives built their own chapel in 1835 on "the old barracks" in the poorer east end where weavers lived and laboured. "The old barracks" isn't a military reference but instead comes from a French word "baraque" meaning "hut or shed". This suggests that those weavers who weren't abiding in the luxury of damp subterranean rooms dug into the riverbank were existing in temporary tumbledown shacks. In such conditions, served by two pubs – the Emerson Arms and the Otter and Fish – and a couple of beerhouses, drink was liberally consumed.

Mrs Maynard took her message to the heart of the community, firstly with her chapel and then by forming the Hurworth Teetotal and Prohibition Society which held its first gala on the village green on Whit Tuesday 1852. Quickly the gala became the social highlight of Hurworth's year and who, in all honesty, could have resisted the allure of the 1861 soiree, which was addressed by Dr FR Lees of Leeds?

The Darlington Telegraph said the guest speaker was "the great expounder of the Temperance question", and it reported: "Dr Lees, in a most masterly and comprehensive speech of an hour-and-a-quarter, reviewed the whole phases of the great temperance movement: Entomological, Scientific, Experimental and Biblical."

The 1863 gala was attended by 1,000 people – many of them day-trippers from Darlington and beyond – who were drawn to the sound of the brass band and the sight of the cricketers on the green.

With such sizeable support, the society wanted permanent premises. In early 1864,

The Road to Rockliffe

it engaged 26-year-old GG Hoskins – the clerk of the works on the great Pilmore Hall that Alfred Backhouse was building – to design a Temperance Hall.

Joseph Pease laid the hall's foundation stone in March 1864 "with great éclat" almost opposite the ranters' chapel, and with great ceremony the hall was opened on December 27. "The weather was magnificent," reported the Darlington Telegraph. "The sun shone brilliantly on the clear frosty atmosphere, so that the village and the surrounding scenery seemed to have put on holiday garb."

It continued: "The style of the building is of a most effective Gothic character, and something quite new in this country." This was Hoskins' first commission. He combined cream and red bricks to lift his austere exterior design, while around the ceiling inside he painted "appropriate temperance mottoes...beautifully illuminated in the mediaeval style".

They weren't so much mottoes as essays: "A good cause when violently attacked by its enemies is not so much injured as when defended injudiciously by its friends...A man's first care should to be to avoid the reproaches of his own heart; his next to escape the censures of the world...Temperance is that by which the real enjoyment of what is good can alone be obtained... No evil propensity of the human heart is so powerful that it may not be subdued by discipline... To thine own self be true, and it must follow as the night the day – thou can'st not then be false to any man."

The hall cost £650 to complete, plus £175 to buy the land. "The building is one which on the whole reflects the greatest possible credit on its talented architect, Mr Hoskins," said the Telegraph.

The Temperance Monument in Hurworth churchyard. It has now lost the bowl on its top

The day-long celebrations began with a morning parade through the village led by the architect and Alfred Backhouse followed by the Northallerton Temperance Brass Band. When they reached the hall, Alfred was persuaded to chair the opening ceremony. Temperance was obviously a cause close to his heart. One of his rare public utterances as a member of the Board of Health was on the possibility of a ban on the sale of alcohol in all Darlington, an opinion that did not endear him to the

Drink

anti-Pease publicans who were pursuing him through the courts as "the illegal member". The opening in Hurworth forced him to make another public pronouncement, albeit brief. He congratulated the villagers and the architect, and, as reported by the Telegraph, he concluded: "I think drunkenness is the greatest curse that inflicts this nation, and the greatest misery that it has to suffer. I trust, however, that the efforts you will make in the cause will be beneficial... The hall certainly is a signal success. (Cheers.)"

The opening was followed by a bazaar, a public tea for 150 people followed by a public meeting for which "the hall was again crowded even to inconvenience". Long religious speeches promoting temperance were made, including one by a Mr Johnson, a Temperance Missionary, who said the new hall "will be like an Armstrong Gun – it will blow down the signs of the public houses in the village".

After this success, the society moved to more practical methods. In November 1878, Alice Scurfield, the lady who erected the animals' drinking fountain at the crossroads, built the Onward Coffee Tavern almost opposite the hall at a personal cost of £1,200. Onward Taverns were spreading quickly across the North-East on the back of the temperance bandwagon and also because of the trendiness of the new tastes of coffee and cocoa. Hurworth's Onward was the first in the district – Darlington's first arrived three years later.

The Darlington and Stockton Times explained the need for the Hurworth initiative: "The attractions which the public house has for young men, and the consequent temptation to imbibition of intoxicating liquors, with the habits of intemperance induced thereby, have been a matter of regret to many benevolent people. Various methods have been attempted as counter-attractions, but from various causes these have not been so successful as could be wished. One of the principal reasons for their failures has been the dull and altogether uncomfortable

A very old photograph of Hurworth looking east past the rounded churchyard wall towards the "old barracks" where the Temperance movement first gained a footing

The Road to Rockliffe

The coffee palace, left, is now a dental surgery, and GG Hoskins' Temperance Hall

character of the substitutes, which have had the effect of repelling, rather than inviting customers."

The Hurworth tavern set out to be attractive. Downstairs was a reading room with all the latest newspapers; upstairs was a billiard room and a library. Chess and draughts were encouraged, gambling was banned, but smoking was reluctantly allowed. Most impressive of all were the kitchens, in which were brewed "the large cups which will contain the beverage which cheers, but not inebriates, to do good to thirsty souls". To get the purest water, a 12ft well had been bored beneath the tavern. Water was drawn up it to the top of the house where a covered cistern contained 1,000 gallons.

Membership of the tavern was five shillings-a-year for adults and three shillings for 15 to 18-year-olds. On the opening evening, 18 gallons of coffee were sold, and Miss Scurfield, assisted by Mrs James E Backhouse, of Hurworth Grange, personally waited on the 56 workmen who enjoyed a celebratory dinner.

The Onward Coffee Tavern marked the high-point of the temperance movement. The tavern lasted a decade, and is now a dentist's surgery. The last name was inscribed on the churchyard memorial in 1902, and the Temperance Hall closed in November 1920 and is now the village hall. As an Armstrong Gun, it proved unsuccessful – the three public-house signs that it threatened to blow away are still swinging.

24: Low Hail Bridge

IT IS a long way from Madison County, in the US, to Hurworth on the road to Rockliffe, in England, but the two are linked by a bridge. Low Hail Bridge crosses the Tees at the eastern end of Hurworth. It is still a private bridge, and walkers are officially advised to use the ancient ford beneath it. In times gone by, it is said that only the gentry were allowed on the bridge and the peasants had to wade across below. The gentry, therefore, tended to hail the peasants low down in the river with their instructions for the day's work – hence "Low Hail".

A better explanation is that in comparison with Hurworth's clifftops, the farmland on the Yorkshire side – a "hale" was a plough handle – is low-lying. Hence "Low Hail".

In the 1870s, Low Hail Farm was owned by General Sir Henry Robinson-Montagu (1798-1883), the 6th Baron Rokeby, of County Armagh, whose family seat was Sandleford Priory, in Berkshire.

Lord Rokeby enjoyed a lifetime of fighting – he was at Waterloo in 1815 and in the Crimea in 1854 – but in 1879, he came to an extraordinary agreement with the villagers of Hurworth. They, in the natural course of their day-to-day business, produced large amounts of effluent which they had to pay the nightsoilman to take away; his lordship had his farmland at Low Hail that needed fertilising. Together, they agreed to go half-and-half on the £2,000 cost of a bridge which would take the human waste from where the villagers didn't want it to where Lord Rokeby did.

The bridge was constructed by Robert Robinson, of Beechwood, Darlington, who also built the carriagebridge over the Tees at Alfred Backhouse's Pilmore estate. Whereas Pilmore appears to have been an expensive ornate and unique design, Low

A postcard with a 1912 postmark showing Low Hail Bridge

165

The Road to Rockliffe

A modern picture of the private Low Hail Bridge at the east end of Hurworth

Hail looks to have been an off-the-shelf American design which was patented in 1820 by an architect called Ithiel Town, of New Haven, Connecticut.

US bridges of this period are characterised by their diagonal trusses, which distribute the weight evenly, and they are often held together by wooden pegs. Ithiel Town's design proved popular because it could be easily slotted together by cheap, unskilled labour. But because these bridges were made solely of wood, they were very vulnerable to rain, causing the deck to rot. So the Americans built cheap wooden roofs and sides to keep the rain out.

This form of bridge-building died out before the 19th Century ended, and today the Americans are very proud of their remaining rustic, rural covered bridges. Indeed, a gently-romantic novel called The Bridges of Madison County, by Robert James Waller, has sold more than 60 million copies. It tells of a photographer on an assignment to capture the nostalgia of the area's famous covered bridges. He asks a woman for directions to a bridge. She is a lonely Italian war bride; he is gritty and handsome. The rest is...

Clint Eastwood directed the 1995 film version of The Bridges of Madison County. He also starred as the photographer with Meryl Street as the woman who knows the whereabouts of the bridge.

Of course, Clint Eastwood has never asked directions to Hurworth's Low Hail bridge. Indeed, Low Hail was never covered and was built of iron rather than wood. But it was built to the same design and if you look carefully at the bridge today, you will still see a large pipe underneath the carriagedeck although it no longer serves its original purpose.

25: Newbus

DOWN a narrow tree-lined avenue towards the centre of another large loop of the Tees stands an ancient house shrouded in secrecy but nonetheless touched by scandal. Newbus Grange, inbetween Hurworth and Neasham on the Rockliffe road, was built in 1610 with big boulders from the riverbed. No one knows why it was called Newbus, and only very little is known about its early days

In 1812, its owners followed the fad for breeding gargantuan cattle and found a degree of fame with the Newbus Ox. It was not as famous as Comet, but it had its moment in the shorthorn spotlight.

Newbus' 15 minutes of fame came in 1894 when it was bought for £8,500 by Captain Robert Allison Brown. He spent a further £27,000 "remodelling the estate", adding castellations, turrets and large leaded windows to the 17th Century grange.

Unfortunately, the money he used for the work was not his.

In April 1904, he was called before a public examination at Durham Bankruptcy Court and a sorry story unfolded. It emerged that a few years before the purchase and the remodelling, Capt Brown's father-in-law, Christopher Applegarth, had died leaving £42,000 in trust for his two young children to inherit when they came of age.

Newbus Grange, from a 1962 sale catalogue

The Road to Rockliffe

In his role as trustee, Capt Brown set about "investing" the money. He bought the Rock Colliery at Spennymoor and £40,000 worth of shares in a Middlesbrough engineering firm, Harris, Thomas and Co. He also lavished huge sums on Newbus Grange.

But the Rock Colliery collapsed, and Harris, Thomas and Co began haemorrhaging money. In fact, Capt Brown even found himself as guarantor for the company's growing debts.

Plus, of course, there was Newbus Grange. Capt Brown admitted in court that he would not recoup the £8,500 he had paid for the estate, let alone the £27,000 he had spent remodelling it. Indeed, in 1962, Newbus sold for about £35,000 – the same amount the Captain had spent on it nearly 70 years earlier.

His slide into bankruptcy was complete when Christopher's married daughter, Mrs Mary Hunter, came calling for her £14,000 share of the trust fund.

The Darlington and Stockton Times concludes its coverage of "the affairs of Capt RA Brown" with a disappointingly inconclusive paragraph: "He was allowed to pass his public examination at the Durham Bankruptcy Court on Tuesday."

However, Capt Brown is believed to have finished his days in a debtors' prison, and even before the hearing was complete, the Grange had been auctioned to Captain Charles Hylton Joliffe. He set about creating the best herd of shorthorn cattle in England on the estate. He was also a keen angler, and planted a row of apple trees along the riverbank so he could have some sustenance while he sought salmon. Those trees still stand.

Capt Joliffe sold the estate in 1920 to Captain Sydney Riley-Lord, another great cattle breeder. The Riley-Lords came from Gosforth. Sydney's grandfather, Sir Riley Lord, joined the fledgling Prudential insurance company in 1856 at the age of 19 and rose to command its North-East operation. He was Lord Mayor of Newcastle and was knighted by Queen Victoria for his services to the city.

The Riley-Lords' time amid the panelled splendour of Newbus was in many ways like Lord Southampton's down the road in Rockliffe: it was the last hurrah for gloriously upper-class England. There was a nanny for the four children, a lady's maid, three housemaids, a parlourmaid, a butler, a cook and a kitchen maid. There was a swimming pool, tennis courts, a croquet lawn, a squash court, a Bentley in the garage, and social life revolved around the hunt and racehorses – the most famous winner being Babur in the Lincoln Handicap in both 1957 and 1958.

Although Capt Riley-Lord's indefatigable daughter, Miss Scylla Riley-Lord, was extremely well known locally – when she followed in her father's footsteps and became the High Sheriff of Durham, she was the first woman to hold the position – the family sold Newbus shortly after his death in 1959. It stood empty for 15 years before being converted into a hotel, and now Brown's folly – another splendid piece of eccentricity tucked away in a loop of the Tees – is making its way as an independent hospital for people on the autistic spectrum while its grounds have been turned into a quiet, riverside caravan park.

26: Neasham and the Headless Hobgoblin

AFTER curling around Newbus, the River Tees develops a curious kink, like the profile of a face. This, then, is Neasham, "the estate by the nose-shaped bend", according to its Anglo-Saxon name. There is a far more fanciful derivation which only dates back to 1800 when a woman rolled her skirts up above her knees and paddled across the river. Shocked to see such a flagrant flaunting of bare flesh, a man on the bank shouted: "Shame! Shame!" The woman, in an eloquent turn of phrase, raucously replied: "'Tis nae shame." And so we have Neasham.

Water-based stories abound at Neasham because, of all the settlements along the Rockliffe road, it is the one that has been the most troubled by the temperamental Tees. Even one of its very earliest inhabitants had a watery grave: in 1939, the 15,000-year-old skeleton of an elk was discovered in a brickworks. Archaeologists reckoned it was an elderly animal that had become stuck in the shallow riverbed and had drowned. They concluded that because there were remnants of fertile vegetation in the peat bed surrounding it, it had died in the warmer period that immediately

Hurworth Hunt at Neasham Abbey, painted by John Ferneley in 1846. The Hurworth Hounds were originally kept on Hurworth Green by Robert Colling – one of the brothers who bred Comet. In 1803, the hounds were bought by the Wilkinson brothers of Neasham Abbey, and Hurworth Hunt was born. The hunt was a major attraction to the early 20th Century sportsmen who lived down the road in Rockliffe

The Road to Rockliffe

followed the Ice Age. The Neasham Elk – which would have been a complete skeleton had it had the requisite number of antlers – is a rarity. Only one other elk skeleton has been found in Northern England, and no evidence of elks has been found any further south.

While archaeologists have been able to study the physical proof of the Neasham Elk's existence, they have struggled with certainties concerning the Headless Hobgoblin of Neasham. Hob Hedeless, to give him his name from days of yore, infested the road running from Hurworth to Neasham, but due to some strange character defect, he was unable to cross the Kent, the beck which runs into the Tees at Neasham.

Hob was a kelpie, an evil spirit, who sat by the side of the Tees and lured women, children and easily-led men into his sub-aqueous abode where – and history is contradictory at this point – he either ate them whole or caused the river to swell above its usual levels so that they drowned.

The Headless Hobgoblin became public enemy number one when he was heavily implicated in the death of Robert Luck, a Darlington bricklayer, on December 31, 1722. Luckless Robert was said to have encountered old Hob as he travelled from Hurworth to Neasham that New Year's Eve. People at the time blamed his drowning on the evil spirit, overlooking the possibility that he might have been overwhelmed by New Year's spirits. They gathered together to have the treacherous Hob exorcised. He was laid under a large roadside stone for 99 years and one day and anyone who sat on it was glued to it forever.

The road between the villages was relaid about the turn of the 1800s and the stone

An Edwardian postcard showing the east end of Neasham

was fearlessly removed. The disturbance did not encourage the Headless Hobgoblin of Neasham to re-commence his reign of terror. In fact, in the modern days of floodbanks and streetlights, he is not known to trouble the inhabitants at all.

The one historical story about this village which does not include water is probably the most important: the founding of Neasham Abbey by Lord Dacre, Baron of Greystock. He received a charter from Henry II (1154-89) and began construction work in 1203. The abbey was dedicated to the Virgin Mary, and was home to eight Benedictine nuns. They were not all wholly godly women for on one occasion they were admonished for their bad behaviour, and when it was discovered that they had pawned their altar cloths, they received another good ticking off from their Benedictine bosses.

Through gifts, the nuns acquired pockets of land all over the North-East – it is surmised that one of their granges, or grain stores, was the first permanent settlement within the Pilmore loop of the Tees – it was the original Hurworth Grange.

In 1534, Henry VIII dissolved the monasteries. Three of his men, with local hired help, demolished Neasham priory, making the five nuns homeless. They were granted an annual pension of 28s 6d while the prioress, Jane Lawson, was allowed £6pa and her family bought for £277 and five shillings the bits of the abbey's estate that the king didn't fancy.

The Lawsons ran out of male heirs after a century, and so for more than 200 years the estate was bought and sold on by a variety of families until it was purchased by the Wrightsons, the Teesside engineers. They built "the abbey", a house, which stands today at the western entrance to the village.

Just along from the abbey are Neasham's two fords: High Wath, the oldest, and Low Wath. The Ordnance Survey map suggests that both are still crossable to Eryholme on the Yorkshire bank, although High Wath was put out of use by the effect of illegal sand and gravel removal from the river bed in the 1950s.

About 300 years earlier, it had been put out of use by a different sort of illegal action: highwaymen. The Neasham waths were fairly important crossing points for the Great North Road over the centuries, particularly if the bridges were down or especially if the traveller wished to avoid the tolls. Indeed, High Wath was traditionally the spot where the people of Durham welcomed their new Bishop as he entered his diocese for the first time from the south. Mid-river, he was presented with the famous falchion with which brave Sir John Conyers slew the Sockburn Worm (see Chapter 27). An eyewitness described the arrival of Bishop John Cosin in 1660: "As soone as the Bishop came in sight of the banks, the trumpetts sounded and the gentry, with the troops of horse, all in one body, judged to be about 1,000, moved into the midst of the river, where, when my Lord came, the usual ceremony of delivering a great drawne falchion was performed, after which the trumpetts sounded againe, and great acclamations of the people followed; which ended, they proceeded in order to Darlington."

The Road to Rockliffe

A souvenir postcard of the Tees in flood at Neasham on June 10, 1914

In the latter half of the 17th Century, three Neasham likely lads – Messrs Barwick, Middleton and Copperthwaite – employed spies to watch the waths and to tip them off when a wealthy potential victim was approaching. Bishop Cosin was so wary of their activities that he advised a business associate in Yorkshire not to cross that way carrying money. The Bishop wrote: "Mr Hilton's son, who brought your letter hither, tells us he was in great danger to be robbed about Darnton and Neesum by thieves and highwaymen that lay upon the street there, to set upon passengers who they thought carried any money with them; and he named Barwick for one, a famous thiefe, with others in his company, besides one Middleton, and one Copperthwaite, who layd at Neesum for their prey, and that he was putt to ride full speed for four miles to escape them."

A little later, another bishop and two of his companions were physically assaulted by the robbers, and this encouraged Durham to invest in repairs to Croft bridge rather than ride the risk at Neasham.

The two waths were not Neasham's only means of bridging the Tees: the third was the ferry, which is still recalled by the Boat House next to the Fox and Hounds. It is thought the ferry ran until 1873. In October 1907 the parish council decreed that the owner of the Boat House need not provide a ferry if they didn't want to, although it suggested that a boat might come in handy. A sure sign that ferry days were over came in 1908 when the resident of the Boat House planted a large post in the riverbank to help foot passengers navigate as they waded through the water.

There can barely have been a resident of Neasham who, at some time in their lives,

Schoolboys throw stones into the rising river at Neasham in November 1960

has not been touched by the water. A letter written in March 1753 told how the great flood the month before "drowned almost entirely all the village of Neesham, having destroyed every house except one, to which all the people resorted, and by good luck saved their lives, though with the loss of all their cattle and stacks of hay and corn".

Sensible villagers would have taken precautions, but instead the Victorians exacerbated the floods. During the 1880s, horses pulling heavy wagons found it increasingly difficult to drag themselves up the steep incline out of Low Wath, so the road through the village was lowered by as much as six feet. This enabled the carts to easily carry on their way but also created a collecting pool for the floodwater.

Over time, Neashamites tired of frequent inundations and in 1970, the much-prized riverside green was moulded into a large grassy bank to keep the Tees at bay, despite local objections that this would be like putting an ugly scar across a delicate nose.

27: Sockburn and the Dragon

THE Rockliffe road pushes deep into the Sockburn peninsula, a narrow finger of land created by the sinuously looping Tees, bringing us to a mystical, magical place where poets fell in love and where a dragon was slain. The broad sweep of history here begins with the Romans, whose Rykeneild Street ran to the east of Sockburn on the Yorkshire bank, not crossing until it reached Middleton One Row. But there was a wath, or ford, across which a traveller could pick his way from Rykeneild Street onto the peninsula where, at some time, an Anglo-Saxon called Socca lived. He had a fortified house, or burg: Socca's burg, or Sockburn.

This, though, was more than any old fortified house because here, "aet Soccabyrig" in AD780, Higbald was consecrated Bishop of Lindisfarne. And here, at a monastery called "Sochasburg", in AD796 bishops Higbald, Ethelbert and Badulf met to consecrate Eanbald, Archbishop of York.

For such significant events to take place, Sockburn must have been an important religious place. It certainly feels like one. It is a peninsula, like Durham. It has a spring – perhaps of holy water. And its prized possession is a tumbledown Saxon church, full of wondrous carvings by skilled stonemasons who mixed Scandinavian mythology with Christian symbolism.

When Aldhun was Bishop of Chester-le-Street between AD990 and AD1018, a chap of Viking descent called Snaculf gave "Socceburg and Grisebi" to the monks of St Cuthbert who were building a cathedral on Durham's peninsula. About a century later, the monks gave the Sockburn estate to the Conyers family out of gratitude for a daring deed performed by brave, brave Sir John…

This story is set in days of old, when knights were bold, and when a terrible monster terrorised the residents of County Durham. It lived on the Sockburn peninsula, and its main weapon was its halitosis – its breath was so pungent that all whom it wafted over died an agonising death.

For seven long years the dragon laid waste to fields for seven miles around, and its voracious appetite was only satisfied by a bath in cows' milk – or by the blood of a pretty young maiden. As James Conway wrote in an 1872 epic poem:

Each morning, from the silv'ry stream,
It crawled, in angry mood,
Until a maiden went to it
With nine cows' milk for food;
But if neglect, or chance occured
To cause the maid delay,
In anger fierce it did devour
All that came its way.

Word of the monster's reign of terror spread far and wide. The bravest knights came from every corner of the kingdom to thwart its evil ambitions, but although many managed to slice through the serpent's body with their swords, its wounds immediately healed. Then it turned on them, its frenzy redoubled, and they succumbed to its all-consuming power.

The king determined to rid his land of the dreadful dragon and sent his champion warrior, brave, brave Sir John Conyers. On the way into Durham, Sir John encountered a soothsayer who gave him two pieces of advice: firstly, only attack the monster when the Tees is in full flood and, secondly, make sure you are wearing armour that is covered in razor blades.

Taking heed, Sir John waited until the snow was melting higher in Teesdale and the river was rising before he ventured out of Neasham onto the long and lonely stretch of land that is Sockburn. On the way, all kitted up in his special armour, he popped into the church for a quick prayer. In an awe-inducing vision, it was revealed to him that if he were to succeed, he would have to offer his only son to the Holy Ghost. Sorrowfully, but without hesitation, Sir John sent his son to a monastery. Then he rode out in search of the lair of the Sockburn Worm.

He found it by the river. The dragon saw him coming and stared at his impudent foolery through its blood red eyes. It blew its noxious breath into his face, and it reared up before him to its full and frightening height. Then it pounced, wrapping itself so tightly around him that it threatened to crush every bone in his body. But Sir John, of course, was covered in razors.

> *Against him, then, it furious rush'd*
> *And twined him closely round,*
> *While his sharp razors did inflict*
> *Full many a ghastly wound,*
> *Until the Tees, as it ran past,*
> *A tempest-swollen flood,*
> *From Sockburn to the ocean, was*
> *Polluted with its blood.*

The vermin now was wounded. But not mortally. Tighter and tighter it squeezed Sir John, forcing his lungs so flat that he feared he would never draw breath again. But then the Holy Spirit entered Sir John's body, filling him with a tremendous energy that enabled him to wield his mighty weapon – a falchion. He hacked away at the dragon with super-human ferocity and bits of its body began dropping into the rushing, flooding Tees.

> *And ever, as the fearless knight*
> *Cut its long body through,*
> *The severed part was sea-ward borne*
> *Ere it could join anew;*

The Road to Rockliffe

> 'Till swept away in fragments small,
> No portion did remain
> Of that foul monster that had wrought
> Fair Sockburn so much pain.

The few bits of the serpent's body that weren't washed away were placed beneath the "Gray Stane", and the people of Durham lived happily ever after.

The tale seems to date from the Vikings of the 9th Century who used the word "orm" – from which "worm" comes – to mean dragon. It may be that in looking for fire-breathing dragons, we are taking it too literally. It may be that there was no dragon with foul air coming out of its mouth. But there could have been a person, an invader, who was spewing foul and treacherous words and laying waste to large tracts of countryside, even raping the womenfolk.

It may be that this invader – perhaps a Scot or a Viking – was only stopped when a local hero bravely drove them from the district at the point of his falchion.

Or perhaps we are trying to read too deeply. Perhaps the tale is true. Sir John Conyers can still be found sleeping in stone in Sockburn church. His triumphant falchion – which dates from the 12th or 13th Century and has the arms of an Anglo-Saxon earl engraved on its handle – can still be seen in Durham Cathedral. The Gray Stane can still be spotted in a Sockburn field near the stone trough where the monster bathed in cows' milk.

And in 1908, near Eryholme on the Yorkshire bank of the Tees just about opposite Sockburn, a fisherman found encased in mud "a huge tooth from the lower jaw of a prehistoric monster". The tooth was seven inches long, two-and-a-half inches wide and weighed 2lbs 9oz. It is incontrovertible evidence that a dragon of some terrible sort perished on this spot at some time.

Sir John Conyers, sleeping at Sockburn

Well, possibly. Undeniably, the monks of Durham cathedral were so impressed with Sir John that they gave him Sockburn peninsula, where his descendants built two houses. The first was a medieval manor; the second was a 16th Century mansion set in parkland. Both are hidden beneath intriguing lumps and bumps of grassland, although four huge blocks of stone survive, carved with the words "SECULOR. . .SOLD.DEO. . .I.MORTALI. . .SECULOR". These words were taken from the Conyers' motto: "Regi seculor. I'mortali I'visibili soli de honor et gloria I'secular secular", or: "To God the only king immortal, invisible be honour and glory world without end". We can only imagine the enormity of the mansion

Sockburn and the Dragon

where once they formed an imposing hearth or an elaborate door lintel. But like Oxymandias' works in the desert, they ended up tumbling down when the Conyers' line ran out of menfolk in 1635.

A poetical reference to Oxymandias would be pretentious elsewhere, but on Sockburn peninsula it is entirely appropriate. Because here, where the great river winds itself almost into a noose, two of Britain's finest poets found their hearts ensnared by a pair of sisters. For one, it was a love that would last a lifetime. For the other, it was a romance that would never quite come right.

The decline of the Conyers allowed others to buy into the peninsula. In the 18th Century, the Hutchinsons came to farm on the western side. In 1785, tragedy struck the Penrith branch of their family, leaving ten orphans. They were posted off to relatives no matter how distant – both geographically and genealogically – for bringing up. And so 15-year-old Mary and Thomas, 13, ended up with their great-uncle in Sockburn. Mary kept in touch with her best Lakeland friends, Dorothy and William Wordsworth. William went up to Cambridge University and got swept up in the French Revolution, during which he fathered an illegitimate daughter. Once the brother and sister had become settled in Dorset, in 1797 they invited Mary to visit.

Wordsworth

Coleridge

For all his philandering in France, William was very fond of his childhood friend, whom he described as "a phantom of delight when first she gleamed upon my sight". His poem continued:

> *A perfect Woman, nobly planned,*
> *To warn, to comfort, and command;*
> *And yet a Spirit still, and bright*
> *With something of angelic light.*

Mary stayed about six months, and met William's new friend, Samuel Taylor Coleridge. The two poets were collaborating on their first publication, Lyrical Ballads, which was to include Coleridge's Rime of the Ancient Mariner. The book was published in 1798 and raised enough money for them to travel around Germany. Wordsworth hated it, and couldn't wait to return to England. But because he had disposed of his Dorset cottage, he had nowhere to go.

So William – an emerging celebrity – and Dorothy asked the Hutchinsons if they could stay with them briefly at Sockburn while they house-hunted in the Lake District. On May 12, 1799, they were met off the stagecoach at Entercommon – a tollbar across the Great North Road abut five miles south of Rockliffe – by Mary's

177

The Road to Rockliffe

A 1927 photograph of Sockburn Hall

brothers, Thomas and George, who pulled them up onto their horses so that they rode pillion over the Tees and onto the Sockburn peninsula.

As they crossed the river, Wordsworth heard the barking of the Hutchinsons' dogs, Dart, Swallow, Music and Prince. All four feature in his poem, Incident Characteristic of a Favourite Dog, in which Dart drowns beneath river ice despite Music's best efforts to save him.

After tea on that first day, the Wordsworths took a short walk around the peninsula and fell in love with its many moods: its pastoral fields, its riverside stretches and its isolated serenity. The brief stay turned into a seven-month sojourn. By day, William walked the river, from the fishlocks at Dinsdale to the east to the grand bridge at Croft to the west, scribbling as he went; by night, Mary would neatly copy out his rough verses.

Perhaps the most famous of the poems that sprung from this time begins:

> *I travelled among unknown men*
> *In lands beyond the sea;*
> *Nor, England! did I know till then*
> *What love I bore to thee.*

It is a homecoming poem about absence making the heart grow fonder – fonder for both country and girl.

As summer turned to autumn, Coleridge arrived at Sockburn. Sparks really flew as around the fire, the already married Coleridge found himself falling for another Hutchinson: Mary's younger sister, Sara. In his sensual poem, Love, Coleridge tells of the moment it happened:

> *She half enclosed me with her arms,*
> *She pressed me with a meek embrace:*
> *And bending back her head, looked up,*
> *And gazed upon my face.*

The house-hunting rides over the Pennines were a success. The Wordsworths had discovered Dove Cottage (now the Wordsworth museum) at Grasmere. What scenes there must have been at Sockburn on the morning of December 17, 1799, when two sets of lovers said their farewells and the men rode off to the other side of the Pennines, Wordsworth working in his mind as he went on a poem – To M.H. – about his last walk with Mary through the Sockburn woods.

Neither poet ever returned to the happy banks of the Tees, but in 1802, Wordsworth married Mary. She became the bedrock of his life. She may even have had a hand in his most famous poem, I wander'd lonely as a cloud.

The Coleridge love story doesn't have such a happy ending. His affair with Sara lasted seven years. In his poem Asra (you don't have to be an anagram expert to work that one out), he called her: "Dear Asra, woman beyond utterance dear!" In 1802, his wife bore him his only daughter and he called her Sara.

As Coleridge slipped into opium addiction, the Wordsworths became increasingly appalled at the way he was stringing poor Sara along. They persuaded her to live with them and she became the third of Wordsworth's women, supporting and transcribing for him.

Back on the peninsula that had had such a profound effect upon one of the greatest poets in the English language, the Blacketts were taking over. They'd made their fortune on Tyneside in flax, collieries, shipping and politics. Their principal residences were Matfen Hall, in Northumberland, and Newby Hall, in North Yorkshire, but they liked the peninsula enough to build a Georgian hall.

It was only short-lived as in 1834, Henry Collingwood Blackett, the third son of Sir William Blackett, built a fourth mansion on the peninsula. This is the mansion that still stands, with his arms above the door and his initials on the drainheads. Around the mansion, Henry built a pleasureground, which featured a bridge over the Tees near the ancient ford. It was designed in 1838 by William Hambley, of London, at a cost of £1,200 (about £1m today). Its powerful pillars were of red sandstone quarried from the riverbed, and its carriageway was carried on Baltic fir timber imported from Lithuania.

Then Henry and his wife, Theophania, turned their attention to the elderly church where people had worshipped for more than 1,000 years. That history didn't suit their purpose. They wanted a romantic ruin so they could gaze upon it from their stately home and muse, like poets, on the passage of time. So, in 1838, they pulled the church down. They left standing only its empty windows to form an evocative silhouette.

To compensate the local people, they built a new All Saints Church at Girsby, high on the opposite bank of the Tees. They even kitted it out with Sockburn's bells.

Henry died in 1856 aged 47. His body was carried for burial amid the ruins he had created by his six oldest labourers. "There was no roof left to echo back the responses to the fine and hopeful burial service, nor any steepled bell to toll the mournful event to the surrounding district," reported a local paper.

The fourth Sockburn Hall built in 1838 by the Blackett family whose coat of arms (right) can still be seen above the door

The journalist was deeply critical of Henry's vandalism of the ancient church – "he did injustice to his naturally good taste and mortified deeply the antiquarian spirit" – but was captivated by the scene before him. "In glorious sunshine, the company stood clustered around the vault, with the solitary yew tree and broad and brightly green park on the one side, and the ruin and hall itself on the other – the river flowing in front," he wrote. "The whole lacked nothing of a perfect picture which JMW Turner would have loved to render."

Theophania remained. She enveloped the peninsula in the cloak of privacy. To deter people from visiting the ancient church, she charged them to use the centuries-old ford. When they kept on coming, she blocked the footpaths – even planting trees across them.

The Darlington Highway Board took her to Durham Summer Assizes in 1867. No resolution. It took her to the Spring Assizes of 1868. No resolution.

It took her to the 1868 Summer Assizes, where she was ordered to reopen the ford and the paths. She refused. She appealed twice, and lost.

The board took her before local magistrates, but still she refused to comply.

Sockburn and the Dragon

Finally, she was ordered to appear before the Court of Queen's Bench in London on January 21, 1869.

Legal costs were mounting. This was not a problem for Theophania with the Blackett fortune behind her. The pecuniary difficulty lay with the public purse, until the Board hit upon a masterplan. It started levying a special rate on the people of the Township of Sockburn to fight for their local footpaths. The larger their landholding, the more they contributed to the court case. As the biggest landowner in the township, Theophania discovered that she was paying the highest rates and so contributing most to the board's legal costs – to fight herself. It brought her to her senses. Days before the hearing, she approached the board with a conciliatory offer.

Still Regina versus Blackett went ahead in London. Theophania's guilt was undoubted, and the Queen's Bench decided she should be fined £400 unless she built at her own expense a bridge "dedicated to the public" over Girsby ford. She was ordered to pay all legal costs, and until she had complied, the paths around Sockburn were to be reopened.

This time she did comply. She paid the sizeable legal costs in September 1869 and the following year, fully at her own expense, the Girsby Bridle Bridge was opened to the public.

A stone tablet on the Durham side records her name, the date, the name of the bridge and of its engineer, Henry Dyke. It doesn't, though, tell the full story.

But here, three-quarters of the way along the peninsula, the Rockliffe road peters out. Although Theophania lost the court case, she won the battle, and her final quarter of the peninsula remains private. A footpath takes over, taking the walker to the Bridle Bridge over the water, and then up a steep ascent to Girsby's isolated church, high on an escarpment with a panoramic view over the looping Tees,

The road has brought us all the way from Croft bridge, the spa resort that was the home of Lewis Carroll, to Sockburn, the lair of the terrible Worm which inspired his

Sockburn's Saxon church, here pictured in 1960, was deliberately turned into romantic ruins in the 1840s by Henry and Theophania Blackett

181

The Road to Rockliffe

The end of the Rockliffe road: Girsby bridge over the Tees which the stone says was built by Theophania Blackett in 1870 so that people could reach the new church

Jaberwocky. It has taken us over rivers, railways and canals. It has taken us past plague pits with the deathknell ringing in our ears. It has shown us sundials created by one man's ingenuity, and it has allowed us to stop for a roadside refresher – of coffee, or something stronger – before encountering the naughty nuns of nose-shaped Neasham.

And, of course, the road has revealed to us the sumptuous mansion and parkland of Alfred Backhouse, "the illegal member", the public benefactor, the lover of Nature, the creator of Pilmore which is now Rockliffe Hall.

Enjoy your stay.

Acknowledgements

It is only a little book, but so many people have played large parts in putting it together. In helping ferret out the initial information, Katherine Williamson and Mandy Fay at the Darlington Centre for Local Studies in the Edward Pease Free Library were, as ever, superb. Many of the pictures within these pages come from the Darlington library collection as well as The Northern Echo archive. I must also acknowledge the Durham County Record Office where there is an album of Backhouse photographs which has done so much to bring Alfred to life.

Ernie Hodgson, who grew up on the Rockliffe estate as his father was Lord Southampton's groom, has been a veritable mine of information, particularly in recalling incidents and a way of life that have never been written down and are now in danger of being forgotten forever.

At Rockliffe Hall, I should like to thank Wendy Benson for her support and interest, and Warwick Brindle and Nick Holmes for helping get the project moving. I should also thank them for their part in taking what was a dying estate on my doorstep and making it live so vibrantly again.

Nick Owen's historical work during the restoration proved invaluable, and Brother Robert Moore was most illuminating in regard to the Order of St John of God, where I also need to thank Karen Gilroy. Dorothy Mounsey ferreted out the superb picture of Rockliffe Hall during the second phase of its construction, and Jeff Dickson of Jigsaw Design Studios in Newcastle did a fabulous job on the cover. I must also thank Northumbria Graphics at Northumbria University for the printing.

At The Northern Echo, without Alan Clarke's technical assistance, this book would never have reached the printer. I am also indebted to Peter Barron for his support and backing, to David Coates for smoothing things along, and to Chris Moran for providing the illuminating maps.

Richard Davies kindly agreed to read the proofs and saved me from myself on several occasions, and I am also grateful to Keith Fenwick for his early reading and perspicacious comments.

Finally, my thanks and apologies in equal measure to my wife Petra, my children, Genevieve and Theodore, and my mum who have endured three long years and lost two summer holidays to The Road to Rockliffe.

Chris Lloyd

Chris Lloyd is the Deputy and Political Editor of The Northern Echo. He writes a weekly local history column for the paper, and this is his seventh book on the past of Darlington and the surrounding area. In 2007-08, he was named North-East Journalist of the Year.

Bibliography

Rockliffe Park: A History of the Landscape, by Nick Owen (unpublished, 2005)
Rockliffe Park, Hurworth-on-Tees, Post-Evacuation Report, by Northern Archaeological Associates (January 2009)
Hurworth-on-Tees: A Sketch and Some Reminiscences, by Edith Katherine Harper (James Dodds, 1908)
A History of Messrs Backhouse and Co, Bankers, by Maberley Phillips (1896)
Backhouses Bank of Darlington, by John Banham (NEEHI, 1999)
The Backhouses of Weardale: Their Botanical and Horticultural Interests, by Peter Davis (Garden History Society, 1990)
The Backhouse Family of Darlington, by F Watson (Sunderland Library transcript, 1962)
History of Durham, by E Mackenzie and M Ross (1834)
History and Antiquities of the County Palatine of Durham, by William Fordyce (1857)
A Guide to Croft, Dinsdale, Middleton, Darlington Etc, by John Gordon (1834)
A Guide to Croft Spa, by Miss D Wilkinson (1866)
Dinsdale and Croft, by Dr Thomas Dixon Walker (1864)
Croft Spa: A Short History of the Queen of Yorkshire Villages, by Edith Katherine Harper (North of England Newspapers, 1906)
The Terracotta Designs of Alfred Waterhouse, by Colin Cunningham (Wiley Academy, 2001)
Alfred Waterhouse 1830-1905: Biography of a Practice, by Colin Cunningham and Prudence Waterhouse (Clarendon Press, 1992)
The Oxford Dictionary of National Biography
North Eastern Railway by WW Tomlinson (David & Charles, 1914)
A History of North-Eastern Railway Architecture, by Bill Fawcett (NER Association, 2003)
A Regional History of the Railways of Great Britain Vol IV, by Ken Hoole (David & Charles, 1965)
Stockton and Darlington Railway 1825-1975, by PJ Holmes (First Avenue Publishing Co, 1975)
History of the Stockton and Darlington Railway, by JS Jeans (Longman, Green & Co, 1875)
First in the World: the Stockton and Darlington Railway, by John Wall (Sutton Publishing, 2001)
The Origins of Railway Enterprise, by Maurice W Kirby (Cambridge University Press, 1993)
The Buildings of Sunderland 1814-1914, by Tom Corfe (Tyne & Wear County Council Museums, 1983)
The Larchfield Diary, by Francis Mewburn (Bailey, 1876)
The History and Antiquities of Darlington by WHD Longstaffe (DST, 1854)
The Book of Darlington, by George Flynn (Barracuda Books, 1987)
Victoria County History of Durham Vol IV: Darlington, edited by Gillian Cookson (Boydell & Brewer, 2005)
Darlington – Your Good Health by Joan A Young (1991)

In Sickness and In Health, by Kimberley Bennet (Darlington Borough Council, 1998)
Annual Reports of Darlington Hospice and Dispensary, 1867-1899 (Darlington Centre for Local Studies)
Memories of Darlington Nos 1, 3, 4, by Chris Lloyd (The Northern Echo, 1993-2005)
Back copies and archives of The Northern Echo, the Darlington and Stockton Times, the North Star, the Darlington Telegraph and The Times
Rural Darlington. Farm, Mansion and Suburb, by Vera Chapman (Durham County Council, 1975)
"The Friends" In Council, by ST Richardson (Bailey, 1975)
The Hermit of Peking. The Hidden Life of Sir Edmund Backhouse, by Hugh Trevor-Roper (Eland, 1976)
Girder Making and the Practice of Bridge Building in Wrought Iron, by Edward Hutchinson (Skerne Ironworks, 1879)
GW Bain: Early Days of Banking in Sunderland (Antiquities of Sunderland, Vol VI, Sunderland Antiquarian Society, 1905)
The Historic Parks and Gardens of Tyne and Wear by Fiona Green (Tyne and Wear Specialist Conservation Team, 1995)
The Cordner Manuscripts Vol 28 (Sunderland Library transcript)
Archaeologia aeliana: Miscellaneous Tracts, edited by CH Hunter Blair (Society of Antiquaries of Newcastle, 1935)
Sporting Days and Sporting Stories, by J Fairfax-Blakeborough (Philip Allan & Co, 1925)
St Peter's Church, Croft-on-Tees, by Sue Chaytor (1989)
A Celebration of Hurworth Grange Community Centre 1969-2009 (Hurworth Grange Community Association, 2009)
Lewis Carroll: The Tender Years Around the North, by Brenda Dame Matheson (Nordales Publication, no date)
Lewis Carroll: Child of the North, by Anne Clark Amor (The Lewis Carroll Society, 1995)
Pilgrimages of Grace. A History of Croft Aerodrome, by AAB Todd (Alan Todd Associates, 1993)
A History of the County of York: Vol 1 North Riding (VCH, 1914)
The History of Northallerton, by Michael Riordan (Blackthorn Press, 2002)
Heighington, by Hilary W Jackson (WEA Darlington, 1990)
Sockburn by Dave Went and Marcus Jecock (English Heritage, 2007)
The Legend of the Sockburn Worm, the Dragon of the Tees, by Paul Telfer (Iron Chest, 1991)
Lives Given in Service 1953-2010 (The Hospitaller Order of St John of God, 2010)

Index

Atkinson, Kenny 111
Ashburne 39 43
Backhouse, Alfred 6 10 40 41-90 111 162 182
   Edmund MP 71 80 81 84
   Elizabeth, of Hurworth Grange (d.1911)74
      80 84 85 89 147 164
   James (1721-98) 34
   James the nurseryman (1794-1869) 43 44
      61 65 66 74
   James Edward, of Hurworth Grange
      (1845-97) 73-4 80 82 83-4
   Jonathan (1747-1826) 19 34 41
   Jonathan (1779-1842) 35 37 39 42 80 128
   Edward (1781-1860) 35 37 39 40 43 71
   Edward (1808-79) 40 43 61 65 71
   Rachel (1826-98) 44 45 61 70 71 74 82 84-6
   Thomas James (1810-57) 40 73
   William (1779-1844) 36 37 42 46 47 73 76
Barclay, banking family 44 74 85
   Eliza 68-9 80
Barnard Castle 22 57 76
Bishop Auckland 18 35 80
Blackett, Henry Collingwood 179-81
   Theophania 179-82
Blair, Tony 103 107
Blondin, the Great 132-3
Bonomi, Ignatius 114
Bouch, Thomas 49
Bragg, Nicholas 76-9
Brindle, Warwick 5 107
Brindley, James 19
Brother George Larkin 102 104
Brown, Cpt Robert 167-8
Byron, Lord 23 120-1
Caine, Michael 70
Canals 19 20 35
Carr, John 132-3
Carroll, Lewis 82 122-127 141 144
Cassel, Sir Ernest 136-40
Castle Hills 27 83
Charles II 90
Clervaux family 118-20
Cleveland, Earl of 37-39 90 92
Coleridge, Samuel Taylor 177-9
Colling, Robert and Charles 142-4 169
Comet 19 29 141-45 167 169

Conyers, Sir John 8 125 128 171 174-7
Cookson, James Sawrey of Neasham Hall 94
Cosin, Bishop John 171
Croft-on-Tees 7 29 113-33 178
   Aerodrome 99
   Bridge (river) 9 10 19 34 39 128-33 134 144
   church (St Peter's) 118-21 122 126-7 131
   House 136-40
   Hall 118
   Mill 133
   Monkend Hall 143-4
   racecourse 116
   Rectory 122-4 126 144
   Spa 16 18 113-7
   Spa Hotel 21 24 30 32 99 114-7 131
   Station 28 29 70 92 93 122 145 148
   Station Hotel 145-6
   Stud 116-7
   Working Men's Club 81 131
Dacre, Lord 150 171
Dalton-on-Tees 10 28 151
Darlington 7 9 18 34 41 42 44 142 159
   Blackwell 47 80 82 95 101 111 141
   Backhouses bank 55 59
   Covered Market 46-48 53
   Fire Brigade 91-2
   Friends Meeting House 80 82 85
   Grammar School 57
   Greenbank 44 79 86
   Highway Board 180-1
   Hospital 79 87-9
   King's Head 16 21 59-60
   Library 58
   Local Board of Health 74 76-8
   Races 116
   school 124 125
   St Cuthbert's Church 76
   South Park 65
   Teacher Training College 79
Dees, William 27 30 31
Dinsdale 7 16 25 26 96 178
Dodgson, Rev Charles 121 122-6
   Charles Lutwidge 121 122-127
   Frances 124
Dragon 8 125 128 171 174-6
Dryderdale 42 68-70 79

Index

Du Boison, Eugene 137
Dunn, Hugh 77-8
Dunsa Bank 16
Durham City 35
Dyke, Henry 181
Eastwood, Clint 166
Edward I 150
Edward II 150
Edward VII 139 140
Emerson, William 156-60
Eryholme 151 171 176
Faverdale 8
Fire, at Rockliffe 91-2
Fisher, Alfred 102 103 109
Fitzroy, Charles Henry, Lord Southampton 90 94-9
Fitz-William, Ralph, Lord of Grimthorpe 150
Floods 111 128-31 172-3
Forester, Cpt William Francis 90-2 104
Fox-hunting 16 92-9
Gibson, Steve 105-11
Girsby 179-82
Gordon, Duke of 13
Great North Road 18
Halifax bomber 99
Halnaby 118 120-1
Hell's Kettles 134-5
Henry VIII 150 171
High Force 7
Highwaymen 171-2
Hindhsaw, Jane, Biblewoman 72 85
Hogg, James 27 30 31 32
Hoskins 54 55-60 162
Hudson, George 121
Hunter, John 158-60
Hunts, Bedale 94
  Hurworth 16 26 94 97-8 169
  Raby 16 26
  Sedgefield 16
  South Durham 94 97
  Zetland 94 95 137
Hurworth 7 10 17 21 84 148-66
  Anthrax outbreak 94
  Bay Horse 151 152 157
  Blind Lane 148
  Church (All Saints) 12 13 22 24 148 149 160 161-4
  Cross Bank 148
  Grange (orig) 10 22 23 24 25 45 103 171
  Grange (Waterhouse) 74 75 81 82 83 84 104 148
  House 152-5
  Low Hail Bridge 17 165-6
  Methodists 161-4
  Onward Coffee Tavern 163-4
  plague 151-2
  Ring Field 98 148
  school 149 153 154
  Scurfield Monument 154-5
  Second World War 98 99
  Teetotal & Prohibition Society 161
  Temperance Hall 57 162-3
Hurworth Place 19 84 98 131 141-47
  Comet 141-145
  Croft House 136-40
  Christadelphian Hall 84 147
  Pig and Whistle 144
  Tees View Cottages 138
Hutchinson, family of Sockburn 177-9
Jaberwocky 125 182
Joliffe, Cpt Charles 168
Kipling, Rudyard 82
Landa, Vince 70
Liberal Party 79
Lombardi, Giovanni Battista 87-9
Maxwell family of Croft House 136-40
Mewburn, Francis 21 24 27 48
Middleton One Row 7
Middleton St George 98
Middleton Tyas 132
Middlesbrough 71
  Football Club 8 10 22 99 105
  Town Hall 58 59
Milbank, Annabella 120-1
Sir Mark 120
Mounsey, Edward Backhouse 71 82 84 85 111
  Dorothy 82 110 111
Newbus 7 11 167-8
Neasham 7 98 151 169-73
  Abbey 10 94 103 150 169 171
Northallerton 27 30 82
Order of St John of God 100-4 105
  brothers' cemetery 104
  Juniorate at Hurworth Grange 104
Overton, George 19
Oxen-le-Fields 134
Pease, Edward 35 37
  Henry 53 54 61
  Henry Fell 79
  Joseph 27 33 57 71 76-7 81 107 162
  Sir Joseph Whitwell 71

187

The Road to Rockliffe

Peel, James 86
Pharoah's Daughter, statue 87-9
Piercebridge 9
Pierremont 53 54 61
Pilmore, garden party 73
  farm 10 22
  bridge (over Tees) 9 10 66-8 73 81 165
  lodge 62 72
  servants 71-2 85
Place, family 118-9, 120-1
Porter, Sir Richard Ker 14 15
Pratt, Margaret 82 110 111
Quakers (Society of Friends) 73 76 79
Railway, East Coast Mainline 19 27-33 122
  Haggerleases 31
  North Eastern 93
  S&DR 19 27 39 128 153
Raine, Thomas Surtees 21-26 33 49 61 148 149
Raby Castle 25 37
Rawcliff 7 10 90
Rennie, John 35
Richardson, Samuel Tuke 73
Richmond, school 123
Ridley, Thomas 32
Riley-Lord, family 168
Riots 29
Riseborough, Thomas 116
Robinson, Robert, civil engineer 66-7 165
Robson family (Darlington) 41
Rockliffe, animal graves 104
  brothers' cemetery 104
  coat-of-arms 51
  Court 104
  cricket club 98
  fire, 91-2
  golf course 107 109
  Home Farm 103
  hotel 105-111
  name change 90
  plane crashes 96 99
  stained glass 102 103 109
Romans 9 30 82-3 109 174
Scorton 101
Scurfield, Col George 152-5
  Miss Alice 155 163-4
Seaham 23
Seringapatam (Srirangapatna) 14
Sockburn 7 8 125 171 174-82
Southampton, Lord 90 94-9
Skelly, Colonel Gordon 11 12-16 21 49 61

Skerne Ironworks 67
Stained glass 102 103 109
Stapleton 133
Stephenson, Robert 33
Storey, Thomas 27 30 33
Storm, Graeme 111
Strikes 51-3
Sunderland 35-36 39 43 44 57 73 91
Sundial 125 157-8
Surtees, family 21 25 45 148
Swan, Col Robert Clayton 91
Tailboys, family 150-1
Tees, River 7 8 11 18 19 118 128-33 148 157 165-6 169 171-3
  Bore 9 10 129
  god 118
  Viaduct 27 30-33 63 66 99 115
Temperance 76 84 161-4
Trees, oaks 62-3
  sequoiadendron giganteum 63-5
Underhand 117
Walker, Dr Thomas Dixon 17 25 28
Walworth Castle 137
Waterhouse, Alfred 47-54 55 56 61 66 69 71 74 75
Weardale 27 41-3 46 68-70 73 156
Weavers 17 18 34
Welch, Henry 27 31
Wellington, Duke of 14
Whitley bomber 99
Wilkinson, George Hutton 27 30
Williamson, Rev Robert Hopper 24 149 153
Winteringham, Thomas 116-7
Wolsingham 69 70
Wordsworth, William 177-9
Wrightson, John, of Sun Inn 76
Zetland, Lord 90 94

188